Spiritual Feasts

By

G. D. Watson

ISBN 0-88019-278-X

Schmul Publishing Co., Inc.
Wesleyan Book Club
Salem, Ohio
1991

Printed in U.S.A.

Printed by
Old Paths Tract Society
Shoals, Indiana 47581

Contents

Chapter	Page
1. The Lord's Feasts	5
2. A Sheep's Journey with the Shepherd	17
3. Palm Tree Saints	29
4. The Workings of the Human Spirit	33
5. Dissolved in Love	40
6. Interior Sufferings	43
7. Full Assurance	48
8. Millionaires in Grace	53
9. Watchfulness	59
10. Dangers to Deep Spirituality	63
11. The Practice of God's Presence	70
12. The Saint's Dressing Room	75
13. Eating the Book	81
14. Three Kingdom Stages	86
15. Holy Ghost Tears	91
16. Anxiety and Faith	96
17. Threshing out Chaff,	101

Author's Preface

Nearly all the chapters and the title of the book were given to me one afternoon in June, 1896, while traveling on the train from Toronto to Detroit. I have not been able to put into the book all the things that I had hoped to, and have had to write out many of the chapters at intervals, amid other pressing labors.

Amid the multitude of books in recent years on Christian holiness, most of them treat of the human side, explaining sin, consecration, faith, and religious duties. A very few of them treat mainly of the Divine side, of the perfection of the Divine nature; and I know of none that expounds the mode of existence of the three Divine Persons in the Godhead.

If reading this book will enable some of God's dear children to understand Him, to love Him, and to worship Him, with a more intelligent and ardent devotion, that will be my ample reward in the day when the Lord Jesus shall come to make up His jewels.

George D. Watson.

CHAPTER 1

The Lord's Feasts

The true Scriptural idea of the worship of God is that of a feast—a banquet of the soul. In the Old Testament the word "feast" is constantly employed for a season of special worship. In the twenty-third chapter of Leviticus the Lord directed Moses to arrange for seven feasts, saying, "Speak unto the children of Israel concerning the feasts of the Lord, which shall be holy convocations."

1. *The Feast of the Sabbath.* Verses 2, 3. "These are my feasts . . . the seventh day is the Sabbath of rest, an holy convocation." There is a prophetic significance in having the Sabbatic feast the first of all, indicative of what is in the Greek Testament called "first day Sabbath." Under the law it was six days of work and then the Sabbath of rest; but under the Gospel it is rest first, and then work. Out of soul rest comes the best kind of spiritual work.

The first day that Adam lived on earth was the Sabbath. Creation was six days old, but Adam was created at the close of the six days. His first day was the Sabbath, a prophecy of the new spiritual creation in Christ Jesus, wherein the believer takes his Sabbath at the beginning of the week. Where our Testament reads "the first day of the week," the Greek is always "first day Sabbath."

There is hardly any worse religious bondage on earth than that of Christians adopting the Jewish Sabbath and making an idol of the seventh day.

A well-fed man can work better than a hungry one, and the feast of the Sabbath of rest was put first on the list, that the soul, being refreshed, might go forth in better service. The prophet Hosea told the Jews, "that God would change their Sabbaths" (Hosea 2:11). The first step towards salvation is to cease from our own legal works, from our own self righteousness, from all merits in what we have done, and lay ourselves down at the feet of Jesus, as lost and undone, in order that He may save us by grace alone.

We never can have our sins pardoned by our own works, and only when we cease from all self-dependence can we accept of salvation as a free, unmerited gift from Christ. This is why the feast of the Sabbath, the cessation from self-works, comes first in those seven feasts, which set forth the various steps and experiences in salvation.

2. *The Feast of the Passover.* Verses 4-8. "In the fourteenth day of the first month, at even, is the Lord's passover." This feast was to commemorate that awful dark night which was the culmination of the ten plagues in Egypt. Every family of the Hebrews was to slay a lamb and sprinkle the blood upon the door posts, that the death angel might see the blood, and pass over that house, without slaying the firstborn; but in all the houses of the Egyptians the firstborn were slain. Hence this feast is the feast of justification, when the penitent soul, having ceased from its own works, flies to Jesus and gets under His shed blood, and is thereby pardoned, and protected from the avenging law. Jesus is our passover Lamb; and in order to escape the wrath of God, we must by faith accept of His sprinkled blood, which constitutes, in the truest and deepest sense, our feast of the passover.

Remember, this feast was to commence in the night, a type that it is always night in the soul of the sinner when he comes to Jesus to get under the pardoning blood. Again, this feast occurred at the beginning of the Jewish year, in the fourteenth day of the first month.

When the Jews left Egypt, God changed their calendar; and in a spiritual way when we leave the Egypt of our sin God changes our calendar, and we begin a new spiritual year with our new life. The first fourteen days of the Jewish year typify days of repentance, of sorrow for sin, and being twice seven, represents the perfection of repentance for all sins.

At the close of those fourteen days from the Jewish New Year came the passover, getting under the blood, prefiguring that just as soon as we reach a point of perfect repentance, we will get under the sprinkled blood of Jesus, and be abundantly pardoned, and delivered from the wrath of God against our sins.

The Israelites left Egypt in the spring of the year, in the latter part of March, and God made it the beginning of their year; for there is a Divine fitness in all the times and seasons of Divine providence, and His dealings with men, both in the outer and the inner life. Every great movement in God's dealings with the world has commenced in the Spring of the year, north of the equator.

Without doubt, Adam was created in the Spring. Noah's flood occurred in the Spring. The Jews left Egypt in the Spring, commemorated still by the Jewish passover and the Christian Easter. The Israelites entered Canaan in the Spring. Our Savior was born in the Spring, about the time of the passover, and not in December as the Romish church fixed it. Then Jesus was crucified in the Spring, on the very day of the passover. Scripture expresses the thought that Jesus will return in the Spring of the year, and Christ intimates in His parables, by the budding of the fig tree we say Summer is nigh, so will it be at His second coming. All of God's thoughts are wrought out on one magnificent pattern, and harmonize in every little detail, both in outward history and the inner life of religious experience.

Hence it is always a spiritual Spring of the year, as well as the beginning of a new spiritual year, when a sinner flies from the Egypt of sin and takes refuge under the precious blood of Christ, the passover Lamb. Thus the feast of ceasing from our own works prepares us for the feast of the passover, or justification.

Another item about the feast of the passover was, it had to be "eaten with unleavened bread." This was because they must needs go with great haste, without taking time for the leaven to rise in the bread. Another reason was leaven is always a type in Scripture of the carnal mind and fleshly reasonings. What an awful blunder it is to hear a preacher announce for a text, "A little leaven leaveneth the whole lump," and then proceed to preach that a little religion will convert the whole world, when Paul in that very passage speaks of leaven as corruption and urges the Church to "purge it out."

Bread without leaven symbolizes receiving Christ, the true nourishment of our souls, with simple faith not mixed with carnal reasonings or doubts. The teaching is a short, quick process, trusting Christ's blood alone, with unmixed faith, before the yeast of our own reasoning has time to act, and thereby sour our trust, or vitiate our perfect confidence in the substitution of Christ for the sinner.

3. *The Feast of Offering the First Fruits, or the Feast of Consecration.* Verses 9-14. "Ye shall bring a sheaf, or handful, of the first fruits of your harvest, and the priest shall wave it before the Lord, and ye shall eat neither parched corn, nor green ears, until the day that ye have brought an offering unto your God." The original word in Scripture for "consecration" is to "fill the hand," that is to take a handful of the first fruits of our new life, new hopes, new joys, new possibilities and lay them down on God's altar, or in our Savior's hands as a pledge, that all we have and all we are shall be His forever.

There is not a single instance in all the Bible where consecration is spoken of as the act of a sinner, or where it is a substitute or a synonym for repentance. Every passage on consecration is addressed to the Lord's people. Hence in the order of these seven spiritual festivals, that of the first fruits, or consecration, is the next one after the passover, or the feast of justification. There are some clear distinctions between repentance and consecration. Repentance must precede pardon, and consecration must precede sanctification.

Repentance is to forsake our sins, but consecration is to yield up to God's will all our good things.

Repentance is to shake off the things of Egypt and leave them, but consecration is to take the first fruits of our new spiritual life and give them to the Lord. Repentance is produced by a wholesome fear of the wrath to come, but consecration is produced by an intense desire to please God and be made holy. Repentance refers to something behind us in the past, but consecration refers to something ahead of us in the future.

Repentance is to let Satan take what belongs to him, but consecration is to let God take what belongs to Him.

The Lord claimed, in a very special way, the first born of man or beast, the first fruits, the first city captured in Canaan, the first of all increase, and under the new covenant the first day of the week. Out of all our substance we should give Him the tenth first; we take the nine tenths afterward, that in all things, as the apostle says, "Christ may have the pre-eminence."

The words about our not eating the bread, or parched corn, or green ears of our first fruits, until we have brought an offering unto our God, signifies that we are not to stop to live on our conversion or the blessed fruits of our justification. But rather,

Just as soon as regeneration grace has brought forth in us faith, hope, and love, we are to hasten to give ourselves up entirely and everlastingly to the Lord Jesus, that we may receive the full inheritance of sanctification by faith, of the fulness of the Holy Spirit. How few of us ever carry out this pattern of the spiritual feasts.

In most cases we live on our religious blessings and greedily appropriate the first fruits of the new life until we are chastised with spiritual poverty, and the wells of grace run low, and our religion seems a failure; until by sad and bitter experience we learn to yield ourselves utterly and live on Christ and not on our experiences. The Lord converts that we may lay our new life absolutely in His hand, to be purified, anointed, illuminated, mellowed, enlarged, and utilized, by the power of the Holy Ghost, for His glory. This is the significance of the third feast, of the first fruits, in the program of our religious lives.

4. *The Feast of the Pentecost, or Feast of the Baptism with the Holy Spirit.* Verses 15-22. The word Pentecost simply means fiftieth. From the time the passover lamb was slain, the Hebrews were commanded to count seven weeks, making forty-nine days, beginning with a Sabbath, and then adding the Sabbath at the end of seven weeks, making just fifty days. On the fiftieth day from the passover they were to offer sacrifices of seven lambs and a young bullock, and two rams, an offering by fire, and then one kid for a sin offering, that is original sin, and two lambs for a peace offering. Now please notice in these various offerings there were sacrifices for actual sin, and then the goat for original sin, and then peace offerings, indicating that the Feast of Pentecost was the time for the thorough sanctification of the soul and filling it with perfect peace and the fulness of grace.

Notice again, that the law was given on Mt. Sinai on the day of the first Pentecost that was ever had. Just fifty days from slaying the passover lamb in Egypt the Lord descended on Mt. Sinai, in clouds, and fire, and thunder, and spake out of the midst of the fire the ten commandments, and afterwards with His finger wrote them on tables of stone. See Exodus 19:10-25.

If you will read the verses indicated describing the first Pentecost, please notice the word "sanctify," in verses 10 and 22, and see how the work of sanctification is connected in every way with the feast of Pentecost. At the first Pentecost on Mt.

Sinai, sanctification was taught from the standpoint of law. At the Christian Pentecost in the upper room in Jerusalem, sanctification was experienced and proclaimed from the standpoint of grace. Just fifty days from the crucifixion of Jesus at the passover the Holy Spirit fell on the believers in the upper room, corresponding exactly to the giving of the law at the first Pentecost. Almost universally people speak of the disciples waiting ten days for the Holy Spirit. This is contrary to Scripture, however, which tells us that Christ was dead three days, and then spent forty days of His risen life on the earth, leaving only seven days for the disciples to wait to complete the fiftieth day, when the Holy Spirit came.

At the first Pentecost the law was given; at the last Pentecost the same law was written in the hearts of the believers, so that they could in deed and in truth keep the two tables of the law, and love the Lord their God with all their heart, and their neighbor as themselves. At the first Pentecost the Lord descended in fire; at the last Pentecost the Holy Ghost descended in the form of tongues of fire. At the first Pentecost Moses ceremonially sanctified the people, and they washed their clothes, Ex. 19:14. At the last Pentecost Christ sanctified the upper room believers in heart and washed their spiritual robes. At the first Pentecost there was the voice of a trumpet; at the last Pentecost the voice of testimony. Thus we see that the Feast of Pentecost, or the Feast of Sanctification, comes next in order after the Feast of Consecration.

Another feature about the Feast of Pentecost, it was to be an expression not only of purification, but of Divine abundance, of the overflow of love, of generosity to the poor and needy. The Feast of Pentecost came at the time of the wheat harvest, and at the time of the ripening of the Summer fruits, about the first week in June. Hence in connection with this Feast of Holiness, it was commanded, "when ye reap the harvest of your land, thou shalt not make clean riddance of the corners of thy field, neither shalt thou gather any gleanings of thy harvest, thou shalt leave them unto the poor and the stranger." The feast of the Passover or justification came at the barley harvest, very early in Spring, hence the Egyptian barley harvest was destroyed in the ten plagues, and the Hebrews crossed the Jordan about the same time of the year, during the barley harvest.

But the Feast of the Pentecost came fifty days later, at the full ingathering of Summer grain and Summer fruits.

How perfectly God's providence arranged all this, as setting forth religious experiences, that we should have a Spring harvest of graces in our justification, but a full multiplied harvest of the graces and fruits of the Spirit in our sanctification, when we receive our personal Pentecost, and the full baptism with the Holy Spirit. The very thought of stinginess, littleness, scarcity, is utterly repulsive in connection with the glorious incoming of the Comforter to drench and overflow the soul with whole seas of joy and love and peace.

How appropriate it was that God should positively prohibit anything like penurious gleaning of the fence corners in connection with the feast of Pentecost. That was a time for the overplus of both Divine and human love, when there should be great handfuls of corn, and wheat, and figs, to give away to the poor Jews and the strangers from the Gentiles who might be traveling by. Hence Pentecost stands for the abounding fulness of salvation, graces to give away, liberality for the poor heathen, an overflowing heart, and an outflowing purse, and a widening mantle of charity unto the distant parts of the earth.

5. *The Feast of the Blowing of Trumpets, or the Feast of Holy Testimony.* Verses 23-25. "In the seventh month, in the first day of the month, shall ye have a Sabbath, a memorial of blowing of trumpets, an holy convocation."

This blowing of trumpets sets forth very clearly the sounding of the tongue of fire in testimony to the cleansing Blood of Jesus and being baptized with the Holy Spirit. It corresponds exactly with the words of our Savior. "Ye shall receive power after that the Holy Ghost has come upon you, and ye shall be witnesses unto me, in Jerusalem, and in all Judea, and in Samaria, and unto the uttermost parts of the earth." It also agrees with St. John, that the saints "overcame Satan first by the blood of the Lamb, and secondly by the word of their testimony."

The old Methodists had their love feasts when all the classes came together for a general praise and testimony meeting, to sound forth the high praises of God, and rehearse what great things the Lord had done for them. Such meetings were well named, for the Holy Spirit had said thousands of years ago that following after Pentecost there should be a feast of testimony and of blowing the Lord's trumpets. This feast is still perpetuated by those believers who have had their Pentecost, and who make up the first-born Church, that elect number who will compose the Bride of the Lamb. Christian testimony to Christ's cleansing blood is a most unpopular feature with worldly professors, but is earth's sweetest music in the ears of God and the Heavenly hosts. The testimony of the saints is like the sweet golden tasseling of a field of corn, the sending forth of the fragrance of the bread of life.

If you put a sea shell to your ear, you will hear a faint roar coming out of it, as if it were bearing testimony to the deep sounding sea from whence it had been taken. And in like manner a heart that has been sanctified in the depths of the Savior's blood, will, like the sea shell, sound forth its memorial of praise and thanksgiving unto all generations.

6. *The Feast of the Atonement, and Affliction of Soul, or the Feast of Suffering with Christ.* Verses 26-32. "On the tenth day of the seventh month, shall be a day of atonement, and ye shall afflict your souls. Whatsoever soul it shall be that shall not be afflicted in that same day, shall be cut off from among his people." Three times over in these verses occurs the command of affliction. What can it mean, that following the great joyous feasts of Pentecost, and blowing of trumpets, there should come this harsh command, thrice over, of "soul affliction?" And yet mark you, it is a feast, and just as truly a feast as any of the others. Can we find anything like it in the life of Jesus? Let us see.

Our Savior was baptized by John in Jordan, which corresponds with His feast of the first fruits, or the abandonment of His young life to the will of the Father. Then there descended upon Him the Holy Spirit, which corresponded with His Pentecost. Then the trumpet tones of the Father's voice from Heaven bearing witness to Him corresponded with His feast of the blowing of trumpets. And then followed the unspeakable conflict with Satan in the wilderness, and that threefold temptation to His bodily appetites, to His mental faculties, and to His religious nature, in which we are told that "He suffered being tempted." The same order of experiences comes in the lives of all God's saints. After great blessing come great testing and trials, and the feast of "soul affliction" follows invariably upon the overflow of the Pentecost and the trumpets.

The sanctified soul must pass through manifold trials and

temptations, which put to an everlasting test the deepest principles of the moral nature. The three great powers of the soul, faith, and hope, and love, must in detail be tried in the furnace and united to God in a life of pure faith. When glass and steel come in a liquid form from the furnace, and are rolled in the solid form they are to take, they are then put into another furnace to be *annealed* so as not to crack, and to stand any temperature.

In like manner, God takes the soul after sanctification and *anneals* it in the furnace of trial in order to fix all the graces in perpetuity and qualify it for any emergency. Nothing on earth brings persecution like testifying to the sanctifying Blood of Jesus, and this is another soul affliction following the feast of blowing of trumpets.

Abel was killed for bearing testimony. Joseph was sold for telling his dreams, and testifying against the wickedness of his brethren. Jesus was crucified, not for being holy, but for testifying that He was God's Son. The apostles were whipped for their testimony for Jesus.

The Romish inquisition killed fifty millions of Protestants for testifying that they were saved without praying to Mary. All religious persecution is against testimony. Hence in the very nature of things, in a fallen world like this, the feast of atonement, of sorrow, of soul affliction, follows next in order after the blowing of the trumpets of a Pentecostal testimony.

There are many souls who draw back from the bitter herbs of this "feast of afflicting the soul." After being baptized with the Spirit and giving a few blasts from their trumpet, when they find that they are to follow Jesus in the wilderness, and endure scorn, and privation, and loneliness, and misrepresentation, and it may be manifold desolations, either in their outward lives or their inner experiences, refuse to obey the command to afflict their souls. They are like the glass plate that cracks in the annealing furnace, though it may be used for some inferior purpose, yet fail of the high prize of a place among the bridehood saints. The word is "whatsoever soul it be that shall not be afflicted in that same day, he shall be cut off from among his people." He will fail in his rank.

When sanctified people turn sour under persecution, and go about fighting and scratching and clubbing God's true people, they only show that they have been cracked in the annealing furnace of the sixth feast, and are losing their place among the perfectly pure, and gentle, and dovelike souls who make up the Lamb's Bride. Unless we are determined to be dissolved in the love of Jesus, and with a lamblike spirit bear all things, endure all things, believe all things, and hope all things, we shall never get successfully through the feast of atonement and of soul affliction. Jesus was baptized three times; first by water, and then by the Spirit, and then by death. The feast of atonement is the baptism into death, into suffering with Christ, and no one can endure that in the full Scripture measure until after they are baptized with the Holy Spirit.

When the mother of James and John requested Jesus to give them a high rank when He should return and reign on the earth, He did not say, could they receive the baptism with the Spirit, but could they receive the baptism of death, which corresponds with this feast of affliction, and which is the ordeal, not of being saved in Heaven, but of measuring our rank in the coming kingdom, and in the Lamb's Bride. It is one thing to frequently talk about these things, but a thousand times more to actually go through this feast with the Smyrna saints.

7. *The Feast of Tabernacles, or the Feast of Gladness and Praise.* Verses 33-44. This was the last of the great annual feasts, at the time of gathering in the last of the harvest, and corresponds with our American day of Thanksgiving. This feast was to commemorate the gladness and the rejoicing of being delivered from Egyptian bondage, when they had not as yet had time to make any tents, but built themselves booths out of palm branches and willows and other green boughs that they found growing in Arabia.

"The fifteenth day of the seventh month shall be the feast of tabernacles. And ye shall take you on the first day of the week, the boughs of goodly trees, branches of palm trees, and the willows of the brook, and ye shall rejoice before the Lord your God seven days. Ye shall dwell in booths, that your generations may know that I made the Children of Israel to dwell in booths, when I brought them out of the land of Egypt." Just as the command in the sixth feast was that "they should afflict their souls," so the command in the seventh feast was, "they should rejoice before the Lord." After the night of weeping there was to come the dew besprinkled morning of praise.

How perfectly this order of the feasts is still wrought out in the lives of the saints! After a baptism of sorrow, there comes the baptism of joy. There is a feast of joy in justification following the bitter pains of repentance. There is also an inexpressible gladness following the suffering of heart crucifixion of the carnal mind. This same order is perpetuated and expanded on a larger scale when the sanctified soul has followed Jesus in the furnace of trial, and humiliation, and manifold testings, and sufferings, and come forth into a marvelous life of Heavenly detachment, and boundless charity, gentleness, sweetness, and Divine gladness.

We must not only die to all heart sin in the Feast of the Pentecost, but in passing through the Feast of Soul Affliction we must die to a great multitude of things that in themselves are not sinful. We must die to friendships, to attachments, to religious plans, to what are called sanctified ambitions, to our own experiences, to our own best judgments, to creature love, to beautiful ideals, to our own good works, to things both inward and outward, to things in the past, and things in the future. We must die to our sorrows and failures, until the soul is Divinely detached and gently floats upward, like a detached balloon, in that boundless ocean of azure sky, where it sweetly floats in God as in a sea of crystal love and compassion. There its whole life is constant adoration and praise for God on the upward side, and compassion, charity, and intercession on the downward earth side.

Up from the indescribable trials of the sixth feast, the soul goes forth into a beautiful green forest, and lives under the rustling of palm branches, and green boughs, and the sway of willows by the brooks, with the dew on the grass, and the sweet voiced birds singing everywhere, and the cloudless sapphire skies pour down noiseless streams of peace and rest, deeper than words, and broader than the vision. This is God's picture of the feast of tabernacles; the feast of the ripened harvests of the Christian graces; the feast of maturity in a life of love; the feast of everlasting song that crowns the work of the precious Blood. Of all the seven feasts, this is especially the one selected by the Holy Spirit to be perpetuated in the millennial age, when Jesus and the glorified saints shall reign over the nations, after the awful scourging of the great tribulation.

These seven feasts set forth, on a stupendous scale, the history of our world as well as individual experience. The millennium will be the world's feast of tabernacles, the seventh feast in the seventh thousand years of human probation. If you will read Zechariah 14, please notice the following words, and the order in which they come. "The Lord shall go forth and fight against the nations. . . . And His feet shall stand in that day upon the Mount of Olives. . . . And the Lord our God shall come, and all the saints with Him. . . . And the Lord shall be King over all the earth. . . . And everyone who is left of all the nations (who were not killed in the tribulation) shall go up from year to year to worship the King, and to keep the feast of tabernacles." Three times it is said, the nations in that day shall keep the feast of tabernacles.

If these words do not mean literally just what they say, then they mean nothing at all. When the sanctified believer comes out into his feast of tabernacles, he has a preliminary taste of the millennium, and it becomes the tranquil joy of his life to look for the coming of Jesus.

CHAPTER 2

A Sheep's Journey with the Shepherd

Of all the various expositions of the twenty-third Psalm which I have read and heard of, the most satisfactory one to my mind was opened up to me one day as a spiritual biography, or a journey which the believing soul takes with Jesus through the various changes of spiritual scenery in a life of faith.

It is not unlike a journey from the Eastern portion of the United States to California, in which we travel through the level pasture lands like Illinois, and then cross the rivers of the Mississippi and Missouri. We then ascend the high plains of Kansas and Colorado, then pass through the dry canyons of Arizona, (Arid— dry, resembling the testings of faith) and then the olive and orange groves and fatness of California, where the cup of bounty runneth over.

Let us itemize the steps of experience in this Psalm, which pictures forth the religious journey of the sheep with their Shepherd.

"The Lord, Jehovah, is my Shepherd." The very first sentence starts with the assurance that you are a sheep, not a goat, and the assurance that Jehovah is your Shepherd, and that you and the Lord are in beautiful harmony and reconciliation. *"I shall not want."* There is the assurance that just as long as we remain in our relation to God, Jesus, our Divine Shepherd, will provide for us, that our souls, our bodies, our lives, our welfare, for this world and for the world to come, will be provided for by our Shepherd. And this expression, "I shall not want," is not the result of reason or of argument, or of outside opinion; it is a Divine conviction that God Himself puts into the heart of the sheep.

The sheep has the consciousness that Jehovah is its Shepherd, and while that relationship remains that the Shepherd will provide pasture and all needful things for that soul. You know the Holy Ghost gives us an assurance of pardon, or of cleansing, or of Divine providence, or of God's care over us, and it is an inwrought persuasion, wrought in the heart by the Holy Ghost. It is not simply popping up and saying, "The Lord is my Shepherd;" it is a Divine inwrought consciousness of relationship with God, by which we have the unswerving conviction that, because we belong to Him, He will not and cannot forsake His own.

2. The next step in this biography is, "He maketh me to lie down in green pastures." This represents entire consecration, entire, unlimited, everlasting abandonment to our Lord Jesus Christ, and this is wrought in us by the Lord Himself. *"He maketh me to lie down."* The soul does not make itself lie down. It has to be willing. It has to cooperate with God. But the Holy Ghost prompts the believer, moves the believer, to the spirit and the act of entire abandonment to God.

The very posture of lying down at the feet of Jesus represents giving up everything to Him, all the past, all the future, all we know, and all we do not know. It represents casting all the burden, all the anxiety, all our affections, all our dispositions, at the feet of Jesus. It is the posture of entire weakness, entire helplessness, entire abandonment to God Himself. This comes as a result of the new birth, the very fact that we are His sheep, and He is our Shepherd, showing that entire consecration to Jesus comes after the new birth. Just as repentance must precede pardon, and be a condition of receiving pardon, so entire abandonment, yielding ourselves to God, must precede and prepare the way for sanctification, for the reception of the Holy Ghost.

"He maketh me to lie down." You cannot make a sheep lie down if he is hungry, for a hungry sheep is fidgety, nervous, restless. You must feed him to make him be still. Neither can you make a sheep lie down if he is scared. A scared sheep is the most foolish thing in the world. He will jump overboard from the deck of a steamer into the sea; he will jump into the fire, into the ditch. When sheep are frightened you cannot do a thing with them unless you catch them; then they become still. This shows us that the sheep has such confidence in the shepherd that he can lay aside all anxiety about wolves and bears and dogs, and because of his confidence he is willing to lie down and keep perfectly quiet and still.

We never go into the fulness of entirely yielding ourselves up to God except on the basis that we have confidence in God that He will manage everything and take care of everything. See how we act as long as we are fussing and fidgety and carrying our own burdens, trying to manage things, to manage a church, to manage ourselves, governing our tongues, or our tempers. It is only when we have sufficient confidence in Jesus Christ that we can wholly turn ourselves, and the management of ourselves, everything, over to Him. It is only then that we get still. So the sheep lying at the feet of his shepherd represents the very act, the very spirit of us having unlimited trust in God. This is the spirit of consecration, both inwardly and outwardly, in the act, and in the spirit of the act.

"He maketh me to lie down." Oh, how many times we have to learn that lesson. We learn it, and then we go and live awhile and then go and learn it over again. It is not that we have broken our entire consecration, but it is the weakness and frailty of our nature. Even old saints, who have been given up to God for many years, have to learn over again, to come back to Jesus as a child and lie down at His feet. When we come to die, if we do before Jesus comes, what is it but lying down at the feet of Jesus. When we see Him in Heaven, what will it be but to gaze into His face, and then lie down at His feet. What a picture of the soul's utter helplessness! Oh God, teach us forever and forever to lie down, to give up. You have got to do it! You cannot manage yourself. You cannot manage other people. Give up and lie at the feet of Jesus.

3. The next thought is the locality where He makes us to lie down. There is a topography of the soul just the same as there is of the earth. Jesus picks out the place where we are to consecrate—where we are to lie down. The sheep do not pick it out. There is a geography in the soul life just as really as there is in the earth. It is like taking a journey across the earth, mountains and rivers, and rocks, and shadows. And so there are certain places where God picks out for us; there are certain junctures, certain times in your life where God can make you lie down, when He could not in certain other places, because the circumstances were not conducive to it.

God picks out the step to get converted, and He picks out the crisis to get sanctified. He picks out the friends, and the books, and the meetings, and the hymns. God superintends all the circumstances to give us what help we need. In green pastures we must let God choose for us. This is the very essence of consecration. Let God choose our field of labor, our place in the kingdom, in the church. He does not want every single child to be doing the same thing or the same piece of work at the same time.

The margin says, "where the grass is tender." We would think that the tall, rank grass would be a good place to lie down. Sheep always go where the grass is fresh and shortest. I have seen horses and cows many a time leave the rank grass and go off in some place where it was just a few inches long. You do not cut down your old asparagus, you take the young asparagus. And so the cattle and the sheep prefer to lie down where the grass is tender. You see, they go by a given instinct.

He knows best the food we need. We want things tall and big—great circumstances, great big words and books and wonderful splurges. That is what we would choose. It is all mere puff balls many times. God picks out little things, simple things, sweet and juicy things, a little prayer meeting, a little friendship, a little touch of blessing. And so God puts the little, short, tender grass beneath us, that is full of nourishment. So the Lord chooses for us. Many times we have picked out the place to get blessed, and failed.

4. The next step is where He leads the soul that is perfectly subdued, perfectly humble, that lies down. That represents the state of teachableness. He takes the soul and leads it right to the baptism with the Holy Ghost. *"He leadeth me beside the still waters."* They represent the Holy Ghost, the river of the Holy Spirit.

The blessed Holy Ghost is compared to a pure river of water from the first pages of the Bible to the very last chapter. There is one river unending that meanders all through the Scriptures from Genesis to Revelation, spoken of by prophets, Psalmists, apostles, and Jesus, the Jehovah Shepherd. When He gets us so conquered and subdued that we are still, He will lead us right to the fulness of the Holy Ghost. But in connection with this leading of the soul to the river of the Holy Ghost, I want to call your attention to the conduct of the three persons in the blessed Godhead, as to how they lead the soul.

The three persons in the Godhead each one lead us in turn. God the Father takes the soul in repentance by the ministry of the law. John the Baptist was a preacher of the law, a type of the law. He was the last minister in the Old Testament. He was the minister, not of the Lord Jesus Christ, but of God the Father. It was God the Father Who sent John the Baptist to prepare the way of the Lord Jesus. And Jesus says that no soul can come to Me except the Father, which sent Me, draw him. I wish you would notice that from the days of Abel until now, never a single soul on this earth has ever taken one step toward the Lord Jesus, except that soul was drawn to Jesus by the Father. Mark the words of Jesus, "No man can come to Me except the Father, which sent Me, draw him." Now, you see God the Father by conviction for sin leads us to Jesus.

When Jesus receives us, He saves, He forgives us, He washes away our guilt, He takes away the burden, He becomes our Shepherd. He makes us quiet, He makes us peaceful. He makes us lie down, and He leads us right on to the Holy Ghost. Now you understand from this twenty-third Psalm what that means, *"He will lead me beside the still waters."* Just as God the Father, through the ministry of the Spirit leads us to Jesus, He leads us to the Holy Ghost and His fulness.

Notice the conduct of our Savior after saving the disciples and many of the early believers, and telling them they were His own flock, that they were not of the world as He was not of the world. He said, "There is something else to come. I am going away, but you tarry in the upper room and wait until you receive the promise of the Father, the river that I have spoken to you about, for I have told you that out of your own heart should flow rivers of living waters. Now you tarry until I send that river upon you, until you get the gift of the Holy Ghost."

On the day of Pentecost the Holy Ghost came upon those believers under three different emblems. One was wind, which typified the gift of life. The other was water. The word water is not mentioned in the 2nd chapter of Acts, but implied literally, "and they all overflowed with the Holy Ghost," which represents the river of water. And then the fiery tongues upon their heads, to illuminate, and empower, and make them burning witnesses for Jesus. So there was the wind, and the water, and the fire. They represent the various manifold operations of the Holy Ghost, to regenerate, and sanctify, and illuminate and impel the soul.

Thus, you see, Jesus was the Shepherd, but His shepherd character was in His nature. And from the skies He reached down that long Shepherd's crook and was leading those sheep. And when the Holy Ghost fell on them, there was a mighty, Divine Mississippi river that struck their spiritual lives.

When the Holy Ghost comes and possesses the believer, what does He do? for remember, there is nothing stationary. When He gets the heart of the believer, He sanctifies it, and takes out the original sin, doubt, fear, jealousy, and revenge. And then He leads that sanctified soul back to God the Father and God the Son. He leads it back, and begins to reveal to that sanctified soul such new visions of God the Father, such charming, sweet visions of Jesus, such an insight into the eternity of God, the immensity of God, the operations of God, the Fatherhood of God, the special providences of God, the beauty of the Divine nature of Jesus.

Oh, how the Holy Ghost opens up the landscapes of Divine things to your spiritual eye, and reveals to you God the Father and God the Son! And then after a while the Father will, in a higher form, a higher capacity, lead you afresh to Jesus. And Jesus will lead you afresh to the Holy Ghost. And the blessed Holy Ghost will, on a still higher plain, lead you back to the Son. And thus the soul is forever climbing a spiritual stairway from God the Father to the Son, and from the Son to the Holy Ghost.

What a wonderful journey God takes the soul on from the time we become His sheep if we submit to Him! We are forever traveling the journey through the mighty labyrinths of the Godhead, without ever sounding the bottom, or ever reaching the end, or finding the measure. What a blissful life in the ages to come to travel around and around in the perfections of God, and always getting fresh views, and stronger joy from God, just to swim and bathe in God forever and ever. Now I say that all this is suggested by this expression, *"He leadeth me."*

It is by the Holy Ghost that our nature gets restored back to God. Do not you see that every word in this Psalm logically follows each other. You could not transpose those words. You could not take one word and put it in advance of its position. When you touch the river, the Holy Ghost restores your nature back to God, your mind, your will, your life, your influence, your thoughts. You know it is the Holy Ghost Who unites us to God. It is the Holy Ghost Who unites the Father to the Son. The Father and the Son have communion with each other through the eternal Spirit.

I wish God would reveal to all His people the glory of the Trinity, the blessedness of the three persons in the Godhead, and how they are produced, and how they act. God the Father loves Jesus, and Jesus loves the Father. It is the union of these two loves that produces the Holy Ghost. From eternity the Father must love His only begotten Son, and from eternity the Son must love His Father. The union of these two constitutes the third person in the Godhead, the Holy Ghost. So that it is by the Holy Ghost that the Father and the Son work together, and commune. Hence, the Bible pronounces "the love of God the Father, the grace of the Lord Jesus Christ, and the communion of the Holy Ghost."

Now then, just as the Holy Ghost in the Godhead is that Divine person whom the Father and the Son commune together, so the Holy Ghost is that Divine person who touches us and touches God, and brings us in communion with God. And all the communion you ever have with the Father or with the Son is through the operation of the Holy Spirit. This is His work in restoring your soul. It not only means restoring the backslider; it means more than that. It means restoring the fallen soul back to the bosom of God, restoring our faculties back to God's faculties, our nature back to God's nature, and that is done when the Holy Ghost takes possession of us.

The next step, *"He leadeth me in paths of righteousness for His name's sake."* Here comes the practical outworking of the sanctified life. You have become a sheep, have laid down at the Shepherd's feet, have been restored to communion with God. Now comes the outward manifestation of that life, and the word "righteousness" refers to the outward activity of the sanctified soul. The word Holiness refers to your inner life. Holiness is a state of your nature produced by the cleansing Blood. Righteousness is a condition of the outward life. And so righteousness means right doing. It is a life of prayer, a life of goodness, a life of benevolence, preaching, writing, giving, talking, suffering, bearing burdens, bearing persecutions, doing all the good you can to the souls of men and the bodies of men, trying to make things right within you and around you. These are the paths of righteousness. You have now got in communion with God by the Holy Ghost. Jesus now leads His sheep in paths of righteousness; here comes in the labors, the prayers of the outward life, just running out into every day practice.

Note, *"For His name's sake."* What does that mean? The name of Christ is His glory, and "for His name's sake" means for His honor, for His Kingdom, for His majesty. And now, then, you are to walk in paths of righteousness for His glory and for the honor of God. You are to labor and suffer and give of your money, your toil, your prayers, that you may glorify Jesus, honor Jesus, spread the kingdom of Jesus. Thus you see you are led in these outward paths for His glory's sake.

Another peculiar thing in this spiritual biography—while the soul is now walking in these paths of righteousness there will come a time when Jesus will lead that soul into great straits and great trials, and severe tests, troubles, and difficulties that cannot be understood or explained, mysterious problems in the mind, heart, and life, difficulties either on the inside or on the outside. And so the soul, while walking in the paths of righteousness, will be led right straight down into the narrow valley, into the deep canyons where every virtue and every grace and especially faith is tried to the center.

And so follow the words, yea, while I am walking the paths of righteousness, while I am following the Shepherd, *"though I walk through the valley of the shadow,"* I will not fear. I want to show that that verse does not refer to physical death. Do you know, all down the ages almost every one thinks that that verse means physical death? That may be referred to. But you will see from the very structure of the Psalm that it does not mean physical dying.

In the first place, how does the soul get into this valley of the shadow of death? By being sick? No. David says the soul gets in there by walking in the paths of righteousness. It is this that puts you there, not sickness. Then again, if this Scripture referred to physical death, when the soul got through it, and got out, it would be in Heaven. And when the Christian dies and enters Heaven, does he find any enemies there? But this man goes into the valley of troubles and comes out on the other side and finds his enemies there. He finds a table and a banquet spread in the wilderness, right in the presence of the devil and his enemies. Now this proves that it does not mean physical death. This valley of the shadow is the experience that the sanctified go through in this life.

The soul is traveling upon a journey. The soul having laid down by the river, and been led through the great, green pastures, it now can ascend to the mountains. And so the Lord says, He leads me through the valley of the shadow of death. Jesus does not lead us into real death, but the valley of the shadow of death.

The soul gets into this narrow canyon, and at two o'clock in the afternoon the great, cold shadow of the rock falls over it and the sun is seemingly down. It is like night in the canyon. The mountain is not fallen on the traveler, the lion is not allowed to tear him to pieces, but the shadow of the rock, and the fear of the lion, falls across the lonely traveler. It represents that, after you have been sanctified, the Lord will lead you through experiences which agree exactly with this statement. You may lose property; it may be disruption among the church members and church fellowship; it may be temptations which are strange to you; it may be difficulties in your mind; it may be spiritual problems you cannot solve. Or God will allow a chain of circumstances to come around you which you cannot understand. Or He may allow your soul to go through certain testings which will try your faith in God to the uttermost.

He will lead you where you can no longer live on the green, tender grass. You will wonder what in the world ails you. You were once by the "still waters," but your soul has been traveling on to more rugged phases of spiritual life. You are now led into things that are more sublime. You do not shout like you used to. You do not pray as you did once. You do not seem to have the freedom you did have, and you guess you have backslidden. The devil tells you, and the ignorant Christians tell you, that you have lost your sanctification, and you go to the altar. You have no more conviction than a plank. You go because you think you must do something, and still you have just the faith in God you ever had. Your emotions have evaporated, and your trials have modified, while traveling on through this valley. Even when you are asleep you are growing in grace.

Now, as you go through this canyon of the shadow of death, you have to die to a great many things in detail which you did not understand how to die to when you first got sanctified, to a great many kinds of folks, and to good preachers, and to wonderful things, and to your own experiences, and to your own sanctification. You get to a place where God shows you your weakness, and where you absolutely have no confidence in the flesh. God is constantly drawing you further and further away from creation dependences, and He is more and more showing you that you must draw your life from God, that you are to live with God, and have fellowship with Him. And so, in this experience of passing through the valley of the shadow of death, it is the deeper death in your own Christian life.

Now while the soul is walking through this valley of the shadow of death, what does it do? It says, in that condition, *"Thou art with me."* It gets into a place in this lonely canyon where it has to go alone. It learns, more than ever, the personality of God, of Jesus, and of the Holy Ghost. It does not say the church is with me, or my experience is with me, but it takes a place where it says, in spite of the valley, in spite of the shadow, I am looking to God. *"Thou art with me."* The soul comes into deeper union with Jesus Christ than ever. Furthermore, while walking in that valley the soul gets into the place where it feeds more on the inspired Word of God.

"The rod and the staff." The rod and the staff always represent the Word of God. When Moses took the shepherd's rod in his hand it was a type of the Word of God. The Lord said to Moses to throw down that rod, and it became a living snake, proving that the Word of God, as a mere secular thing, or in the hands of secular, worldly men, is a mere stick. But when you throw down this Divine thing, it becomes a living thing. "For the Word of God is living and active" (Heb. 4:12). Then God said to Moses, "You catch up that snake, you catch up that rod, and you go to Egypt and work miracles, turn dust into lice, water into blood." Now that was all done by the rod.

Now, as you go through the valley you are not feeding on the tender grass, you have gotten beyond that. You now have the staff to walk with, and there you trudge along. That walking stick is God's Word, and you draw your bread and your water from that walking stick, that rod.

"Thy rod and Thy staff they comfort me." It is in these testings and these trials and these strange experiences you go through that you are driven to your Bibles. You search the Psalms and the Prophets to find a parallel case with yours, and you feed on the inspired Word of God. It is in trials and troubles that people learn to appreciate the Word of God in a way that young Christians know nothing on earth about. This believer gets into what we call the Holy Ghost state of grace. He draws his nourishment, not from the past, but from the Word of God.

When will I get out of that place, some may be asking? Some stay a few months, and some a few years. You get through when the pure Word of God becomes your soul food, when you get where you can suck honey out of the rock. Well, when you get through, suddenly you are led out into a large place. After you have gone through these testings, here comes your soul enlargement.

"Thou preparest a table before me in the presence of mine enemies, thou anointest my head with oil." Now then this proves that it does not mean physical death. If it were physical death, and you were in Heaven, you would not have any enemies to sit down and look at you eat your dinner.

To confirm this, let me call your attention to the fact that our Savior Himself, our blessed Jesus, has gone through every single step of this journey. When Jesus went from His mother's home to the Jordan, He there found the river of the Holy Ghost. He received the full baptism with the Holy Ghost at His baptism by John. There is where He received the Holy Spirit in fulness as the anointed Messiah. Then what did He do? He walked in paths of righteousness; He moved on to obey God. He had been obeying God, but He commenced to walk in paths of righteousness. Where did they lead Him? Into the wilderness. For forty days Jesus went through the valley of the shadow of death. His whole nature was tried to the uttermost. He was alone. He was enduring hardness and He was enduring conflicts we have no conception of. What did He eat? He ate nothing but the Word of God. And when the devil said will not you make these stones into biscuits, He said, "It is written, Man shall not live by bread alone." When the forty days were ended, and He had gotten through by living on the Word of God, the Lord sent angels and they prepared a table in the wilderness, on the rocks. And the devil was skulking behind the rocks. There Jesus Christ sat down and took dinner, prepared by the Father and by the angels, in the devil's presence.

The Lord leads His saints the way He is going, that is, the Bridehood saints. And so your soul must undergo this conflict similar to your Savior. You are then led out where Jesus gives you such feasts as you could not comprehend or enjoy in other years, right in the presence of the devil. At the time that you got this great feast, it was not in your first sanctified experience. It is the enlargement you have after you have been led through the

Savior's trials and testings.

Abraham was sanctified seventeen years before he offered up Isaac. That was his canyon, and after he went through that valley of the shadow of death, God gave him such enlargement. "Now I know, Abraham." These things are all through the Bible, and you receive them when you pass into the deeper death to self, that deeper crucifixion of the sanctified life. After this God takes you into a large place where there comes a sweetness and a wideness that young sanctified Christians do not understand. Young sanctified people are severe. They have clean hearts but often narrow heads. They think if you do not shout as they do you have not got anything at all.

The anointing of David took place at the dinner table. That corresponds with this lesson. There you have the overflow of the spiritual life, the missionary life, the life that lives for others, the life that pours itself out for the welfare of others.

Now we come to the ending up of the Christian pilgrimage. *"Surely goodness and mercy shall follow me all the days of my life."* There comes what some call the final perseverance of the saints. The Scriptures teach that the sanctified soul comes into the place of Divine anointing where it is definitely assured of its everlasting salvation and glory. In the beginning of the Christian life God is always warning us not to look back, but there comes a place where the soul has the Divine assurance of everlasting glory. And in these words of the Psalmist here there is a conviction that the soul will land safe in glory.

"And will dwell in the house of the Lord forever." That house does not mean the Christian church. That does not last forever. That word "house" refers to that city that Jesus Christ is building for His bride. He has been 1900 years constructing the city of pure gold. *"In my Father's house are many mansions."* While Jesus has been building that wonderful structure for the saints, the Holy Ghost has been down here building the bride. While Jesus is building the cage, the Holy Ghost is constructing the bird. Jesus is the carpenter.

In the eighth chapter of Proverbs we are told that Jesus was the house carpenter from all eternity. Jesus is the world builder from the beginning. He is the builder of the universe. So when Christ takes the place of carpenter down here it is in perfect harmony as the builder of the universe. At the second coming of Christ, the saints will rise from the dead, and the glorified millions of earth are to rise, and the Holy Ghost will lift the church of the firstborn from the grave, and from the earth up into the heavens and put the bride into her palace.

CHAPTER 3

Palm Tree Saints

It is very evident from Scripture that all the different animals are types of diversified human character, and also that the various trees, bushes, and shrubs are symbols of different sorts of people and their various stages of character. In the Bible, there are frequent allusions to strong oaks, olive trees, palm trees, and other species of trees, as types, not only of Christ, but of His people. And it is evident that there is a close analogy between the different qualities of these trees and the various virtues and graces of God's servants.

We read in the Psalms that the "righteous shall flourish like the palm tree," and again that the "blessed man is like a tree (and evidently it means a palm tree) planted by the rivers of water." When I was traveling in Jamaica, where I saw hundreds and thousands of cocoanut palm trees, and one never tires of seeing them, I was forcibly reminded of the imagery set forth in Scripture between the cocoanut palm and the devout child of God. Let us notice some points of likeness.

1. The palm tree succeeds best along the seacoasts and the margins of rivers, where it can get an abundance of water. This is a true picture of a saint planted in the love of God and in constant touch with the abiding Comforter. For the Holy Spirit, in His constant flow through the humble soul, acts upon the faculties of the mind and the attributes of the heart and will, just as a flowing river operates on the roots of a palm tree.

There are chemical properties in the air and in the earth which are essential to the growth of the trees and their fruitfulness, but it is especially the action of water that gathers up these chemical properties and imparts them to the fine roots of the trees. In like manner the Holy Spirit, when He has perfect access to the hidden roots of the soul, imparts all the virtues of Jesus and the love of the Father and the vital forces of Scriptures, producing thereby the highest and strongest form of holy character to God's people.

Sometimes the palm tree is found growing in deserts, but always where subterranean springs are running near the surface. In these instances, such clusters of palms form those refreshing oases which are so acceptable to the traveler. In like manner there are great deserts in the moral and spiritual conditions of mankind. Amid these dreary wastes, where the people forget God, the true saint sends the roots of his prayers down into the hidden fountains of God, and by the Holy Spirit draws up constant verdure and fruitfulness for thirsty and perishing souls.

2. The palm tree is an evergreen, which typifies the constant freshness of a true spiritual life. There are many varieties of trees, such as apple, peach, and pear, which are deciduous, and shed their foliage at the approach of winter. All of these set forth a certain degree of Christianity, but the highest types of spirituality selected from Scripture are set forth by those evergreen trees, such as the orange, olive, cocoanut, and date palm. David expressly mentions this quality of unfading green as belonging to the saint by saying not only that he is "like a tree planted by rivers of water," but that "his leaf also shall not wither," or as the margin reads, "shall not fade."

There are deciduous Christians, and in fact a large majority of Christians live a deciduous life in which the sweet, fresh verdure of grace comes and goes with various seasons of their lives. Only a few of God's creatures are so thoroughly rooted by the river of the Holy Spirit as to have an evergreen life and manifest that sweet, gentle, cheerful, child-like freshness and verdure of soul which makes their presence like a refreshing shade on a hot day.

It requires a supernatural stream running constantly down from the eternal freshness of God through the human heart to keep all the affections and thoughts verdant and fragrant. Every thing human will fade. All flesh-born love, human youth, school-boy sprightliness, mental science, theological zeal, pulpit eloquence, artistic singing, and everything that does not flow out from the Holy Spirit will wither; but a soul that is established in constant prayer and fellowship with God is perennial.

3. The palm tree has its life hidden in the center and not on the surface as other trees. The palm has no bark, and so it can never be killed by girdling it. Most trees have a bark under

which the sap flows, and they grow by an increase of the layers of wood put on every year just under the bark. Hence if the bark is pulled off the tree dies. This girdling represents the life which is yet natural, which can be seriously damaged by outward circumstances, or persecutions, disaster, neglect, or ill usage.

We constantly meet people who live on the surface and know hardly anything of being hidden in a supernatural way with Christ. All their religious experiences are easily affected by outward circumstances, such as large or small congregations, an eloquent or simple preacher, a live or dull prayer meeting, good or bad treatment, riches or poverty, or a little piece of persecution, and such things as belong to the outward form of life.

The palm tree, drawing its life up through the center, especially represents the soul whose life is not dependent upon outward circumstances, but is thoroughly supernaturalized and hid in God. Just as long as a palm tree has enough of its heart left to convey water from its roots to its boughs it will live, though it be cut all around and terribly mangled by the axe. And so a soul that is thoroughly purified and in constant fellowship with the Holy Spirit can endure trials, bad treatment, neglect, persecutions, ostracism, and every sort of calamities in this world, just as long as its inner heart is in unbroken fellowship with the Triune God. This explains why it is that the palm tree never grows in size like other trees, by making additions to the outside of its diameter, but it only grows upward by adding year by year fresh joints on top. Hence the palm tree ten years old will have as much thickness in its trunk as a tree a hundred years old. This beautifully illustrates that the true saint does not grow by spreading himself outwardly in the world, but upward toward Heaven, and making constant additions to his spiritual altitude.

4. The palm tree, and more especially the cocoanut palm, is a constant fruit bearer, blooming every month and always having a cluster of fruit at the top from one year old in age down to the fresh blossom. This corresponds with the Bible statement that the Tree of Life yields her fruit every month. Every Bible reader must have been struck with the way the number twelve is used, such as the twelve manner of fruit, and the fruit ripening every month in the twelve months of the year, and then the number twelve being multiplied by itself making one

hundred and forty-four.

It is a singular fact that the cocoanut palm will average twelve units every time it blooms, that come to maturity, so that it yields twelve units for each month, or one hundred and forty-four for the year, which makes it harmonize precisely with the Scriptural numbers in many places. It is supposed by many that the number one hundred and forty-four sets forth a special company of saints who will compose the Bride of Christ. And it would seem that those servants which make up that chosen company are, all of them, palm tree saints, having all the foregoing qualities of the palm tree.

There is no tree on earth of such constant fruitfulness as the cocoanut palm, and hence it preeminently typifies the most fruitful of believers, who are not only saved and purged from inward sin, but so filled with the life of God as to have the fecundity of the Holy Ghost.

5. The attractive beauty of the palm tree is another distinguishing quality.

It has no limbs, but long, graceful, strong leaves that stretch out from the top, with a beauty and grace and glistening green which makes it an object of beauty and majesty unapproached by any other tree. In this respect it sets forth the true Heavenly dignity, loftiness, gracefulness, and perpetual charm of a deeply spiritual life. The saints who get a vision of the eternal beauty of God, and bathe their minds constantly in the attractive light of the Divine perfections of Him, are those who in a special way manifest the true charm of a holy life.

It is true that it takes the spiritual eye to see the real beauty of a holy life. Yet even the dim eyes of the people of the world can detect a strange loftiness and calmness of Heavenly independence in a holy life, which looks to them somewhat like a spiritual palm tree, waving its lofty foliage in the breeze and presenting a picture against the sunset skies never to be forgotten. Added to all these qualities the palm tree is long lived, and at the end of a hundred years will yield as beautiful foliage and as fine fruit as in its younger years, thus confirming the Word of God, that the palm tree saints will bring forth fruit in old age.

CHAPTER 4

THE WORKINGS OF THE HUMAN SPIRIT

In the religious life there is a middle ground between the direct agency of the Satanic spirit on one side and the Divine spirit on the other. The middle ground is occupied by the workings of the natural human spirit, and makes up a little world of its own, partly good and mostly bad, where all moral principles are liable to get mixed; it is a field of many difficulties and misunderstandings in connection with the spiritual life.

The book of Proverbs covers this territory of the natural operations of the human nature perhaps more thoroughly than any other portion of Scripture. "There is a way that seemeth right unto a man, but the end thereof is death," is one of the natural outworkings of the human spirit left to itself. There is something in the diabolical spirit and in the Divine Spirit so distinctive and well defined in their character as to be easily recognized; but in the multiform movements and vibrations of the human spirit there are so many blendings of the innocent and the evil, the wise and the foolish, the light and the dark, and so many shadings of character, as to render them very subtle and in many ways imperceptible.

We may suppose that in angels and demons the principles of character for good or ill have reached their fixed form of everlasting destiny, and all their features stand out in bold relief like mountains on a clear day. On the other hand, the human spirit is in this life in its infancy, where every type of character is formative and incipient and like the little undulations in the landscape whose features cannot be so readily discerned from a distance.

The human soul is capable of being united to Satan until it becomes thoroughly demoralized; and on account of the fallen state of man and his natural corruption of heart, there are swift and powerful tendencies in the soul to join in the destiny and image of the devil. Also the soul has untold capabilities of union with the Holy Spirit and of sharing the character, likeness, and destiny of the only begotten Son of God. And because Jesus has redeemed us there is given to every human soul a measure of Divine grace to check it from committing sin and encourage it in righteousness. In addition to this, be it remembered, God created our human spirits for Himself and His personal glory, so that our capacities toward God are greater than toward Satan.

After we are converted, the great conflict in religious experience is mostly an internal warfare with ourselves and the natural evil in our nature. And then after we are sanctified, and the first fervors of perfect love have subsided, we find many things in our makeup, in the workings of our natural human spirits even apart from human depravity, which require much study and discipline and adjustment. We find this interior schooling of ourselves into union with the blessed Jesus is not an instantaneous stroke, but a gradual conquest of the mind of Christ brought out in the details of life. Now apart from these extremes of development of the human spirit of sin or holiness, let us for the present take the middle ground and notice some of the manifestations of the natural spirit which we meet with in our efforts to reach an abiding perfection of love.

1. We notice that the human spirit, even apart from Satanic agency, naturally gravitates to ease, idleness, luxury, comfort, self-liberty and the making of ample provision for bodily comforts and enjoyments. This is why human slavery has fastened itself so deeply into human nature and human society, not always because of a devilish impulse, but because those who have the power like to be waited on and have every comfort of life without working for it. It is true that human slavery will always degenerate sooner or later into forms of fiendish cruelty, because it is a principle into which Satan easily builds his nest. But, naturally it comes from love of ease and ample physical comforts.

It is this natural inclination to taking things easy and loving bodily comforts that cripples the soul in its efforts to be holy. And it can so take on the finest forms as to ascend into altitudes of Christian perfection and weaken very spiritual people. It is this human tendency to the love of ease that causes neglect of secret prayer, or of fasting, or the putting forth of steady, heroic efforts for serving God and saving souls.

2. Another natural operation of the human spirit is to be warm and enthusiastic toward certain virtues and graces while utterly sluggish and somewhat repugnant to other virtues and graces. It is this phenomenon in the human soul which causes so much deceitfulness in our efforts to serve God. Everybody is naturally inclined to some good traits of disposition, which renders it comparatively easy to obey certain injunctions of the Scripture. From this natural impulse many conclude that they are making great progress in the service of God, while at the same time there are certain other injunctions of Scripture upon which they seem to have almost no conscience and an indifference of obedience.

For this reason we can never depend upon our natural goodness, nor even what seems to be the holy impulses of our human spirits. One soul is naturally magnanimous, kind, and forgiving, but will be ambitious or sensual; another is naturally intensely moral, and strict in some virtue, but cruel, severe, or penurious. And thus the human spirit naturally presents a moral landscape where hills and valleys, or uplands and swamp-lands, or vices and virtues seem located opposite each other. This shows the necessity of a most thorough renewal of the whole inner nature, not only purging out the evil dispositions, but purifying what seem to be the natural virtues; for even our aptitude to practice some good things needs to be sanctified and filled with Christ.

Sometimes Christians will have seasons of good feelings, and sudden exaltations of spirit, and impulses warm and tender to do certain things for God, or to enter a deeper life with Christ. Supposing that such impulses flow from the Holy Ghost, they make magnificent vows and form lofty determinations of saintly living, not knowing that in many instances this beautiful impulsion to certain virtues may largely spring from the natural vivacity of the human spirit. After awhile they find that impulses run dry and their right determinations get exhausted and yield no permanent fruit. Nothing can be relied upon in the life of the soul except what comes from God. The Holy Ghost inspires us to undertake steps of faith and obedience in a deep, quiet, thoughtful decision, almost unattended with religious emotion.

God's movements in the soul are like great giants, made up mostly of bone and sinew. Great emotion may result from such operation, but as a rule the greatest process of God in our lives starts from what we sometimes call "dry faith." Thus we cannot judge of our progress in holiness by the effervescence of occasional good feelings, or because we are easily disposed to certain good things. We are to measure our conquest by the destructions of those dispositions which we are the least inclined to have destroyed, and by the fulness of those Christ-like traits toward which we are naturally sluggish.

3. The human spirit is instinctively and universally in love with itself, and, without being educated to it, will intuitively look out for itself and mix up the principle of self-love in everything it does. This inherent disposition is not to be denounced as satanic, for it is purely natural. In a pure and infinite way God must love Himself with infinite satisfaction, and by the inherent necessity of His spotless nature He must do all things for His own glory. But this infinite and essential self-love in the ever blessed Godhead is the very foundation of all blessedness to created beings.

The principle of self-love is a necessity in the life of every creature, and the incentive of self-preservation, of wisdom, of seeking salvation, and of all betterment of our being and life. Hence, the wholesale and unconditional denunciation of the principle of self-love is very foolish, and betrays a lack of knowledge of God and Scripture and the constitution of things. But this self-love in a fallen condition is perverted into selfishness; and if Satan is allowed to fasten himself upon it, he may turn it into an instrument of many crimes and everlasting ruin.

Now in the pursuit of entire holiness and unbroken union with God, this feature of natural self-love is to be taken into account, not because it is bad in itself, for it must exist in God and holy angels, yet, because it has been vitiated by sin, it is to be watched with a Divine jealousy. You see, self-love is so fine it can creep into all good works and impair their purity or sap their strength. It is the operation of this subtle self-love that makes us timid, cautious, and over prudent about committing ourselves unlimitedly up to God's will, as if we were afraid God might drown us in the deep sea of His dealings with us.

Then on the other hand when we have yielded fully to God, this same refined self-love makes us over anxious to be great saints, and climb sudden steeps, and stretch our neck for celestial visions, and strain our nerves to make ourselves spiritual heroes. Then again, when we find our ideals are not realized, and we tumble back to the plane of common mortals, we get blue and half despondent and chafe over our defects, like a vain woman fretting over her homeliness, and we are tempted to think that God can never do much with us.

Now each of these phases of experience are accounted for by the one principle of self-love, which, like a chameleon, can change its color to suit every substance it stands upon. It can travel around a whole circuit of religious moods, from grave to gay, from cheerful to severe, and in each instance it will assume the guise of some trait of holiness.

One special form of this self-love is a tendency to talk about ourselves, to magnify our spiritual states, to want others to know our wonderful experiences, a facility for relating our exploits; and then to turn around when occasion suits and bemoan ourselves, pity ourselves, and pour our woes out to other people. All of this springs from self-love, which incessantly seeks to fill the landscape from rim to rim of the horizon with some form of self; either bad self or good self, or sorrowful self or jubilant self. When the soul is dissolved in the love of God it will be instinctively on the lookout for this oozing out of the water of self-love and quickly hide it under the cross of Jesus, and be ever on the lookout to give Christ the pre-eminence and to give others the preference.

4. Levity is peculiarly a trait of the human spirit. Satan may urge gay and thoughtless sinners to laugh and dance themselves into endless woe; yet Scripture never reveals Satan as a being of levity in himself. The starless gloom of eternal night is fastened upon his awful malignant nature, and his very laugh would indicate a fiendish misery. God is essential and eternal love, sweetness, beauty, and cheerfulness. The sacred, awful weight of Divine bliss is too infinite for even the approach of levity or a trifling act. But between the vicious gloom of Satan and the solemn bliss of God, there is in man's nature a levity, a volatility and an outburst of thoughtless, trifling wit, a special human thing. In the state of unfallen Adam, this resembled the pure, innocent glitter of sunlight on the sea, of the rustle of leaves in a forest. But since the fall it is easily turned into an occasion of sin and a great hindrance to progress in solid piety.

There is something in the flow of good humor, sparkling wit, punning, brilliant retort, joking, laughing, trifling talk, which seems so innocent, so far removed from things gross and vicious, that very few Christians get close enough to God to see what havoc it plays in the spiritual life. A wag of a preacher can never lead souls close to God. A mouth of trifling talk can never be the channel of prevailing prayer. It is true the Scriptures give instances of pure wit and playfulness of spirits, and of serious sarcasm, as when Jesus called Herod a fox. But the true spiritual life to be powerful must avoid levity and aimless, foolish jesting. This is what the Holy Ghost means when He says, "In the multitude of words there wanteth not sin."

A soul filled with God is serious but not sad; cheerful but not volatile; firm but not stubborn; gentle but not effeminate; liberal but not extravagant; discreet but not timid; bold but not rash; sweet but not sentimental; elevated but not proud; lowly but not cringing; holy but not harsh. Multitudes of saints, after having been wonderfully baptized with the Holy Spirit, have allowed the overflow of their grand Divine joys to imperceptibly degenerate into mere good humor and social sprigtliness, and effervesce into sallies of wit and jocular conversation, and found their massive locks of God-given strength cut off by the scissors of human levity.

5. I shall mention only one more trait of our natural human spirit which interferes with spritual progress, and that is unevenness, fluctuation of disposition, acting spasmodically and without the long pull of Divine perseverance. It would take a little volume to describe all the traits of the human spirit, such as the play of the natural affections, and the operations of reason, and the office of instinctive human fear, and many other legitimate faculties of the soul which play their part, either as helps or hindrances in the spiritual life; for it is significant that many of the natural dispositions of the human spirit may at the same time be a help to religion and in another respect be a hindrance to it.

But for this chapter we close with a reference to that natrual disposition in every human soul to do things by spurts and spasms. This is a proof of the infancy of man's estate in this world. Notice how children in their play will begin a dozen enterprises in a day and leave all of them unfinished at night. So many begin to repent but never quite give up every sin. So many converted people feel a Divine drawing to perfection and make a sudden and feverish attempt after holiness, but when the crucifixion approaches closely to their heart of hearts they shrink back and fail to die with their Master.

In the truly sanctified state, this quality of unevenness does not entirely cease. We must not regard it as a token of sin, but simply as a trait of that which is purely human. This irregular, corduroy element in our human spirit will inevitably enter more or less into the deepest spiritual life; and while it is not a life of sinning and repenting in the Scripture sense of sin, yet, owing to this human trait, it will be a life in some degree of downs and ups, of shadows and lights, of breezes and calms, of freshening zeal and slackening speed; a sort of life pulse, like waxing and waning moons, or ebbing and flooding tides.

Now like the other human traits referred to there is no sin in this unevenness of constitution, but it may become the occasion of lukewarmness and backsliding. Hence it must be watched and guarded against, and seasons of special prayer are needful that this irregular movement of our human spirit, in its ebb, may not run us ashore; but on the other hand, that its season of rising tide may be so touched by the Holy Spirit as to push us farther ahead toward our ultimate harbor, in the bosom of God.

There will inevitably be downs and ups in the spiritual life, even apart from sin; but to live a real Bible life, the downs are to decrease in their descents, and the ups are to increase in their ascents, for the life of Jesus in us, to be normal, must always be increasing. Thus the Holy Spirit is to teach us how to deal with ourselves, that after being delivered from the touch of Satan, our own human spirits are to be not only saved, but lifted into God and united with the Father and the Son through the powerful working of the Holy Ghost, which worketh in us mightily.

CHAPTER 5

DISSOLVED IN LOVE

While there are thousands of degrees in Divine love, yet there are three stages in our experience of Divine love which can be clearly recognized and somewhat defined.

The first stage is that which comes to us in the new birth, when our sins are forgiven and the Holy Spirit imparts the love of God to our hearts, which constitutes a true conversion.

The second stage is when the heart is purified from indwelling sin, and the Holy Ghost sheds abroad the love of God in the purified soul in such a way that love exists without the admixture of the carnal mind.

The third stage pertains to maturity, to a tried state of faith and love. It is in this third stage of rooted and confined union with Christ that we locate what we mean by being dissolved in love.

The old writers on Christian perfection had much to say about being "dissolved in love," "lost in God," and "sunk in the sea of Divine peace." They uniformly spoke of this state as being one which the soul entered after the first fervors of sanctification, and after the faith had undergone many trials.

When the soul is first converted, the joys of the new birth are so blessed it naturally thinks that it is all taken up with the love of God and nothing else remains in the way of salvation. In a short time, however, it finds the presence of a most positive sinfulness of nature remaining in the heart, and grace has to struggle against an inward principle of self-will.

Then when the believer has yielded himself utterly to God and enters the experience of definite sanctification, the inflow of the Holy Spirit so fills him with Divine love that for a long time the feeling of the whole soul is that of being dissolved in love. In due time God allows this experience of sanctification to undergo many sore trials and testings, both inward and outward, and from quarters not expected. The great battle of

Christian warfare has been transferred from the heart, which is now purified, to the mental faculties.

The outcome of these severe testings to perfect love result very differently, according to the central disposition of the believer. Some of them become severe, harsh, and their very Christian perfection seems to be their greatest defect. Others become lordly and dictatorial, and set themselves up as the only correct teachers of Scriptural holiness. Others under these teachings switch off on some narrow, foolish, unscriptural fad, utterly repugnant to the common sense of intelligent Christians. Others, through these fiery trials, dwindle into discouragement and creep off, as it were, from the battle-field of life into a state of spiritual invalidism all the rest of their lives.

A few of those who have experienced sanctification make their trials and religious conflicts the means of pushing out into the deep sea of fathomless humility and boundless love. It is a terrible delusion to suppose that sanctification is the finishing up of the Christian character. It is more properly the beginning of real Bible character on a supernatural plane. Concerning our being dissolved in love, we note the following points:

1. The first thing about this blessed stage of perfect love is that it must be chosen. It does not come by chance, nor as a matter of course, nor as a mere out-working of sanctification in itself, nor as a careless unfolding of grace. It is a condition that must be deliberately, and definitely, and positively chosen, and prayed for, through thick and thin, through trials and conflicts. The soul must set itself, not only to be freed from sin, but to be melted, expanded, sweetened, and dissolved in the immensity of God's love.

2. When the tried soul is dissolved in love the mental faculties are turned into a gentle, loving action; so that judgments, opinions, decisions, are formed slowly, discreetly, with instructive kindness.

It is one thing to have a clean heart, and a very different thing to have all the faculties so subdued and pervaded with Divine love as to have them act as if by instinct from the heart of Christ. It is a blessed proof of union with God to have the mind moved promptly with the Holy Spirit, to instinctively not only take sides with God, but act with God's disposition and God's charity. To have all the mental faculties act under the power of a kind, gentle spirit, to put the best construction on things, to make generous allowances for others which we dare not make for ourselves, to thoughtfully take the unselfish side, to intentionally look at things through God; in other words, to have all the mind wrapped up in a warm, loving heart, is one of the proofs that the soul is dissolved in love.

3. When the soul is dissolved in love, it will not only make the heart intend to do right, but so over-masters the life as to fashion the manners, words, and conduct, with humility, courtesy, and holy refinement. It seeks to avoid the wounding of others and causing anyone needless pain or sorrov. It is free from that teasing, meddlesome, vexing spirit which some professors of holiness seem especially gifted with. To be dissolved in love, the soul prefers to take the lowest place, to let others have the big end of the bargain, to prefer that others have the honor, and to delight in the happiness and elevation of others, and loves to pour itself out for its fellows. This state is full of the Spirit of encouragement and helpfulness.

It is said of Gregory Lopez that he was so taken up in the love of God that his looks, the expression of his face, the tones of his voice, his words and gestures, expressed such compassion and tender regard for his fellow men that everybody who came in contact which him felt either better or an encouragement to be better. Even incorrigible sinners felt a check to sin after meeting with him. It is the nature of Divine love to encourage, brighten, and lift up; and when the soul is dissolved in love this will be one of its special marks.

4. Above all is our relation to God Himself; and when the soul is fixed in perfect love it will glow with a constant, steady flame of devotion to the three persons in the Divine Nature. Such a soul constantly yearns for the beatific vision of God's face; it ever thirsts for more love; it constantly runs out in gratitude for God's mercies, and makes all its interests one with the interests of God. Such a soul always apprehends its life as indentified with Christ, and makes God the end of all things, the blessed, peaceful harbor toward which all its life and labor is moving.

CHAPTER 6

INTERIOR SUFFERINGS

There are just as many grades of suffering among souls as there are grades of living among men. Suffering may be physical, or spiritual, or all of these blended in thousands of different forms and degrees.

When a soul abandons itself entirely to God, with a perfect intention to be conformed to Jesus, then the Holy Spirit in a peculiar way establishes a disciplinary government over it. He takes charge of every form of suffering such a one may have, whether outward or inward, and so saturates every incident, and trial, and grief, with the providences and purposes of God as to make it work for good to that soul.

The true Christian life is the life of the cross, but the way of the cross is the way of crucifixion, the way of pain, the way of mysterious and unaccountable trials, the way of delicate and keenest suffering. To use the word "cross" in any other sense is only a poetical myth, suitable for light-headed and trifling professors of religion, but not for thoughtful and serious companions of Jesus.

It does not matter from what quarter spiritual suffering may have its origin, if the soul is truly yielded to God the Holy Spirit will gather up every thread of pain and weave it through His loom into a gorgeous pattern of the life of Christ.

Let us now not speak of outward calamities and sufferings, or of the sufferings of the rebellious and disobedient, but let us notice a few forms of interior suffering which belong essentially to a spiritual life, and which every soul must have if it makes the perfect transition from self to God. I say these sufferings are essential, because the transition from self into perfect union with Christ must involve such inward crushings, and grindings, and separations, and meltings, and expansions, and sinkings, and detachments, as of necessity produce strange sufferings in the affections, the will, and the reason.

I am not speaking merely of the heart struggles with original sin, for that ceases when the soul is utterly yielded to God; but I refer more particularly to varieties of soul suffering brought on by the Holy Spirit, Himself, in His sovereign discipline and transformation of the believer.

1. One of these forms of inward spiritual suffering is the sense of utter weakness to accomplish the great task of life. We never see the true magnitude of living until it is revealed to us by the Lord. Very few people get even a glimpse of the huge dimensions of their destiny, or of the solemn grandeur of existence.

When the soul discovers the real task of life, especially of living for God, it looms up like a vast mountain range, with such duties, and privileges, and lofty precipitous possibilities, that it almost takes our breath to think how we can climb those giddy heights, and walk calmly along those narrow ledges, and stand on the apex at last, more than a conqueror. This produces, not so much a positive feeling of pain, as it does a sense of faintness, and a sort of inward trembling, and quivering awe, before the majesty of God's will. But this very quivering of the heart, which at times may be well nigh overwhelming, may be so pervaded by the Holy Ghost as to make the soul bow itself, like Samson taking hold on the pillars of the heathen temple, in a supreme exploit for God.

2. Another phase of inward suffering is that of heart loneliness, by which the soul seems cut off into a strange isolation from other souls. God intends to unite all holy souls in a Divine fabric of unity and fellowship, utterly inconceivable by our natural reason. But before that is accomplished He must take each devoted soul in a private manner off to itself and detach it from all things and creatures, because we have by nature thousands of little threads of instinctive and natural attachments, to localities, and times, and seasons, and persons, and plans, and prospects, and sweet memories, and glittering day dreams, and bright hopes. These threads must be snapped, and the best natural affections must be circumcised, not that they are sinful, but the heart with its thousands of beautiful attachments must be crucified and isolated and as it were islanded away out in the ocean of God, that it may learn in solitude with Jesus how to love like He loves, and be attached to all things and beings as He is, and in the order of God's will.

Hence when the soul is going through this process of great interior isolation it must suffer pain.

We must first die to sinful kinds of love. Then we must die to natural and beautiful kinds of love. Then there are many kinds of religious loves that are not entirely of the Spirit, and these must perish in order that the sweetness, and impartiality, and boundless overflow of Divine love may fill all the arteries of the soul. After we have passed through the sufferings of perfect isolation, and entered the ocean of Divine love, then all the natural affections seem to be born over again, with a gentleness, and sweetness, and immensity in them that we could hardly imagine before.

3. The Holy Spirit will often cause in the purified soul a holy, pathetic sorrow for sin, but without any sense of guilt. An abiding sorrow for sin is a species of holy suffering very needful for spiritual progress. It maintains in the believer the principle of perfect repentance; it deepens humility; it kindles the feelings of gratitude; it keeps the soul in touch with the precious blood of Jesus; it worships the attributes of God; it begets intercession for others, and thirsts for the perfect reign of God, when sin shall pass away from the earth. This sorrow for our past sins, and for the horribleness of past inward sin, and for the awfulness of sin in the world about us, is a blameless and fruitful form of suffering. Under the blessed touch of the Holy Ghost, while it is real inward sorrow, yet it is free from despair, or from despondency, or the least taint of bitterness.

4. A sense of inward pressure, a strange, unaccountable burden, like a sad premonition, is sometimes the form of suffering which the soul passes through in the way of the cross. There are things we pass through in our spiritual feelings which lie entirely below the horizon of our understanding. They are like those storms in summer which are so far away from us that we see no cloud and hear no thunder, but only see little flashes of lightning on the distant rim of the horizon.

Sometimes it seems as if our souls were seized with a giant hand which seems to squeeze us with a strange sadness, or holy dread. Like frightened soldiers in the night we feel for our armor and rush into line of battle as if we had suddenly been charged upon by the enemy. In some this phenomenon takes the form of stifling or strangling, and in others as if being pressed in a vice. Such feeling may result from the attacks of the enemy; but if the soul will keep recollected and give itself to deliberate prayer, such strange inward presure will be followed by a quiet, blessed expansion.

5. Another form of inward suffering is that of having a distinct perception or a presentiment of bitter enmity of others. Sometimes we get glimpses of the awful malice of Satan towards us, and when his relentless hatred is clearly opened to our view, it fairly makes us cry like a little child at seeing a raging beast.

God mercifully hides from us the unimaginable malice of Satan and evil spirits until He gets us close enough to Himself to endure the awful sight, and even then He allows us only faint glimpses that serve to bring us into fellowship with Jesus Christ.

But the Holy Spirit will at times let a true humble soul feel the malice of its fellow creatures. David had distinct presentiments of the bittterness and treachery of his fellows. Madame Guyon felt distinctly the bitterness and deceitfulness of persons who were strangers to her, and the Holy Ghost would put her on her guard not to take to them when she met them. There are times when we distinctly feel the intolerable hatred of people who are hundreds of miles away, and whom perhaps we have never met, and others we have not seen for years, yet there come painful shootings through the heart, like arrows dipped in gall, and a painful sensation that they would crush us into the lowest earth if they could.

This is a real inward suffering. There are facts and phenomena in the spiritual world that are not registered in man's narrow theology. The soul is greater than the body, and has many experiences which are not tabulated in books. This painful sense of being despised by our fellows, even by those professing great religion, when yielded to God in humble, loving prayer will bring us out into a feeling of great tenderness and charity.

6. One of the strangest and most delicate forms of inward suffering is when God seems to fight against the soul, as if He took a rod and beat the inner spirit, until the very soul has a sense of bitterness. Superficial Christians never have this experience; it is for those who are the most utterly abandoned to God. This is the suffering Job referred to when he said, "the Lord seemed to fight against him." And Eliphaz tells us "that we are not to despise the chastening of the Almighty, when He maketh us sore." In addition to all these privations that Joseph

went through in Egypt, we are told in Psalms that "there came a time when the Word of the Lord tried him" (Psalms 105:19). This was the most profound and most delicate suffering of all.

7. God seems to deal with the soul as an enemy until the heart feels bruised to its center, but this is followed with the most exquisite balm.

There is much more fine suffering arising from the great disparity between the benevolent longings of the pure soul and its ability of accomplishment. When we see the spiritual needs of mankind, the destitution of the poor, the darkness of the heathen, the distresses of those in prison and asylums, neglect of religious care of children, and the unspeakable needs of the souls of men, and then see how little we can do, our hearts ache for the world. This is a holy form of suffering; this was one of the sufferings in which Jesus lived all through His thirty-three years, for remember that a large part of His suffering was the limitations of the human nature He assumed.

8. The most beautiful and Heavenly of all our interior pain is that of inexpressible desire for God. There are two great divisions among religious people, those who serve God legally, and those who serve God lovingly. Even among the sanctified there are two classes, those who are severe, and those who are tender. The severe class magnify the legal side of holiness, and these know but little of that longing desire for God that weeps and sighs for His ocean fulness. The tender-hearted saints magnify personal love for God, and they get such bright visions of the person and character of God that they often long for Him so unutterably that the heart fairly breaks with sweet seraphic pain to be lost in the shining abysses of His glorious being.

This is a suffering that angels might covet, and yet a real suffering, that has the capability of absorbing all other suffering. To gaze at Jesus, to blessedly despise ourselves, and then to look away from self, with such burning thirst for Christ as to forget our unworthiness, and to pine for Him until the heart trembles with holy yearning, and the breast expands, and the lips quiver, and the hot tears fall, and the prayer is too great for words, and the soul almost faints to be taken up into the bosom of infinite love, this is the sweet suffering of the spouse of Christ when she says in the Song of Songs, "I am sick of love." The saintly Faber sings, "If we were sick for want of love, how swiftly we would move."

These are only some of the interior sufferings in the soul's transition out of self into perfect union with Jesus.

CHAPTER 7

FULL ASSURANCE

There are degrees of assurance in every kind of knowledge. Most people in the world regard religious knowledge as a vague and uncertain thing, whereas it is our privilege to be more certain in our relationship to God than any other kind of knowledge in the world.

There are three departments of knowledge, namely, physical knowledge, which we acquire through our five senses coming in contact with outward forms of matter; intellectual knowledge which, while it includes the knowledge of nature, also adds that of pure reason, such as logic and mathematics; the knowledge of moral intuition, such as the consciousness of personality, identity, the moral sense of right and wrong, of peace or sorrow, of hatred or love.

Most men regard physical knowledge as most certain, but the true philosopher knows that the axioms of mathematics, such as a straight line is the shortest distance between two points, are more certain than the report of the senses. But many of these men discount the spiritual certainties in religion, yet in reality when we enter the realm of the assurances of the Holy Spirit they are more sure to us personally than any knowledge in the world.

The deepest part of our being is the interior immortal spirit, and there is where the Holy Spirit operates and plants the knowledge of Divine things at the very fountain of intuition and consciousness. It is right and appropriate that our blessed Creator Who formed us by His own Word should arrange to make Himself known to us in the deepest and choicest part of our being.

While creation plays upon our outward senses, and our fellow creatures can enter so largely our intellectual department, God alone can fill and satisfy the interior citadel of our being with deep, serene, unquestioned assurances of His nature, His Word, and His ways.

A state of Divine assurance is where the soul is in harmony with God, so that the Holy Spirit can pulsate, as it were, the same thoughts and feelings into the consciousness which are spoken of in the Scripture. It is, in other words, so purging and illuminating the human spirit that it is lifted on a par with the Bible, so that the written word in Scripture and the infused spiritual word, imparted by the Holy Ghost, agree with each other like two drops of water. The Word of God, written on paper, finds a perfect correspondence written on the inner soul. Let us notice some forms of full assurance mentioned in the Scripture:

1. "The full assurance of faith." We are told in Hebrews 10:22 that in entering the second veil into the most holy place for the perfecting of our union with God, "we are to draw near with a true heart in full assurance of faith, having our hearts sprinkled from an evil conscience." That is, we are to appropriate the precious Blood of Jesus to wash out all inward sin, which is the "evil conscience," and enter through the veil of Christ's crucified flesh into the most holy place of Christ's heart life, and rest ourselves on that Divine altar, where all shadow of doubt concerning our salvation, our pardon, our cleansing, and our full acceptance of the Father is removed.

Herein is a profound mystery, how a soul that is distinctly conscious of being guilty, and impure, and full of dreadful forebodings, can actually get out of that state and be thoroughly conscious of rectitude in motive and intent, conscious of a sweet internal purity, and consciously free from all distressing fears. This is a miracle in the moral universe— the highest of all rank of miracles, for it is a miracle in consciousness; yet this is what is wrought by faith in the Blood of Jesus by the Holy Spirit.

2. "The full assurance of hope." We are told in Hebrews 6:11 that after leaving the first principles and going on unto perfection and being made partakers of the Holy Ghost, we are to keep up the same diligence by which we were sanctified, "to the full assurance of hope unto the end." There is a terrible misuse of this word "hope" by many Christians, who, for lack of Scripture knowledge, use the word hope to express being in a state of salvation; hence the common phrase of "having a hope," or "getting a hope," meaning by it the new birth, or heart purity, which is an unscriptural use of the word. The word "hope," in

the New Testament, is used for having a bright anticipation of the glory to be revealed at the blessed appearing of our Lord.

It is true "hope" includes all good anticipations in the future, both for this life and the life to come. But, I say, in the New Testament "hope" is used almost in every case of blessed fulfillments of God's promises in connection with the second coming of Jesus and of His glorious kingdom and reign. In the Scripture above referred to, the full assurance of hope is spoken of in connection with "the inheritance of the promises," and the promise was to Abraham and his seed that they should inherit the earth. The coming of Christ is called by the apostle "that blessed hope." And in Ephesians 1:18 this "hope" is spoken of as something so great that we need a special revelation from the Holy Spirit that we may know what it is.

The full assurance of hope is produced by the Holy Spirit giving us such a clear revelation of the brightness and glory of things to come as to deliver us from all uneasy forebodings as to the outcome of our lives, and the ultimate overthrow of wrong, and the coming reign of the Son of Man, and our glorification with Him, and as to God making all the things in this life work together for our good. When Christians get from the Spirit a clear illumination of Scripture on Christ's return, and the first resurrection, and the bridehood, and the reign of Christ on earth, and then beyond the general judgment the glorious kingdom of the Lamb, and His saints in the ages of ages, it so widens the soul's vision, and mellows and sweetens the heart, and vivifies everything in the Bible, it is like finding a new contentment in religion.

We should pray to have the realm of hope revealed with full assurance to our hearts.

3. "The full assurance of understanding." In Colossians 2:2 the apostle speaks of "having our hearts knit together in love, unto all the riches of the full assurance of understanding, and the acknowledgement of the mystery of God, and of the Father, and of Christ."

This kind of assurance is different from that of hope. It is the revelation of the Holy Ghost acting through the affections upon the intellectual faculties, enabling the mind to have a cloudless spiritual perception of the three persons in the Godhead, and of the personal character and communion of the Father, the Son, and the Holy Spirit.

This is called by the apostle "a mystery," and the word "mystery" signifies something that can never be known except by revelation to the soul. It is true that apart from the special work of the Holy Spirit, people may believe that there are three Divine persons in one eternal essence of being. But it is impossible for us to have an inward spiritual perception of these Divine persons, and of their individual characteristics and glory, and to have blessed communion with them, without a direct revelation to our understanding. This must not be confounded with the work of sanctification, but is one of the effects or fruits of the indwelling of the Holy Spirit. The apostle states that it is out of a condition of pure love that the understanding receives these riches of assurance.

The heart is the primal element in religion, and only when the heart is full of pure love, very lowly and tenderly, can the understanding open to the dazzling, beautiful light of the Father, Son, and Holy Spirit. By this assurance of understanding, including the highest object of all knowledge, it of course takes in other ranges of religious knowledge, such as the infallible inspiration of Scripture, the everlasting existence of the soul, rewards and punishments, and the whole landscape of revealed truth in the light of a cloudless conviction.

4. Full assurance of various kinds of knowledge. There are many directions in which a believer needs settled convictions, a restful and unwavering conviction in matters of prayer, and providence, and the liberty of conscience. And unless we get into such fellowship with the Holy Spirit as to have ascertained convictions, we are liable to become the petty slave of other people's notions and of teasing scruples. No Christian life is so fruitless and disheartening as one that is in bondage to foolish scruples, that is, making a conscience of things the Scriptures do not settle. Over all this territory of conscience God has promised to give each believer satisfactory light and personal guidance. It is in this connection where individual conscience on non-essentials is being treated by St. Paul, that he says, "let every man be fully persuaded in his own mind," or as the margin reads, "fully assured in his own mind" (Romans 14:5).

Weak minded Christians are always locating sanctity in little externals, instead of a heart full of Divine love; hence we hear people talk of being saved from tea and coffee, eating meat, or wearing a beard, or a necktie, or gloves, or eating warm food on Sunday, and many other things in which each one can have the right of individual conscience, but Scripture teaches us no one has a right to fasten on the conscience of others. The whole of Romans 14 is on this subject.

The things we need to get saved from are evil tempers, impure thoughts, harshness, bitterness, resentment, covetousness, tale bearing, deceitful words or behavior, imprudent conduct, murmuring, fretfulness of spirit, dictatorialness, self-conceit, wanting to govern people, selfishness, love of ease, love of praise, extravagance both in living and in speaking, and every other principle that is unlike Jesus. This is the salvation we need, but the external matters of non-essentials are for the individual conscience, and not properly speaking matters of salvation. In regard to prayer, we read in 1 John 3:19 that "we can know we are of the truth, and shall assure our hearts before God, for if our hearts condemn us not, we have confidence toward God that our prayers will be answered."

If we walk close to Jesus the Holy Spirit will gently insinuate in our hearts the things we are to pray most earnestly for, and He will also give us assurances of the Father's will in answering prayer. Oh, that all Christians knew the blessedness of getting their prayers from God, and praying in the Divine will, for this is indeed the beautiful region of heavenly certainties and satisfactory supplication.

We also have instances of assurance in matters of providence and Divine guidance. In Acts 16:10 we read that after Paul had seen the vision of the man in Macedonia, he and his fellow laborers endeavored to go there, "assuredly gathering that the Lord had called them to preach the Gospel in Europe." This is a different form of assurance from that of faith or hope because it involves the conjunction of inward conviction and outward providence, and also it involves the action of the Holy Spirit on the heart and the exercise of enlightened reason. Hence the word "gathered," in the verse quoted: that is, they put together the forbidding of them to preach in Asia, and the vision of the man in Macedonia, and the exercise of a teachable mind, and drew the definite conclusion with perfect assurance.

Now in all these directions as to individual callings, non-essentials of outward life, Divine providence and personal leadings, it is our privilege to be free from bondage, and to be so fully assured as to have unbroken peace, and yet have no theory or conviction of infallibility in the matter.

CHAPTER 8

Millionaires in Grace

He is rich who owns God, but he is richest of all who owns nothing but God.

It requires a special revelation from the Holy Spirit to make known to us the riches which God can impart to the human soul—riches of faith, riches of love, riches of humility and of wisdom, and the inexpressible wealth of the mind of Jesus. God has chosen the poor of this world, rich in faith and heirs of His coming kingdom.

There is a very close analogy between the millionaires in this world's wealth and the millionaires of grace. The same principle by which men pile up wealth, when applied to the spiritual life, will lead the soul into wonderful riches with God. In both instances the accumulation of wealth is an art to be acquired by the mind and habits of the loving will. I do not refer to cases where people inherit a fortune, nor to the instantaneous operations of grace which come at justification or in the work of sanctification. But I refer to the constant increase of wealth, where persons being in poverty learn the art of so saving and investing or trading that they acquire almost a supernatural tact in making money or in making advances in grace.

Where wealth is obtained suddenly, as by accident, the possessor may not know how to manage it, and soon lose it. In like manner, many Christians who are powerfully converted or sanctified depend unconsciously on blessings to keep them. Unless they learn the holy art of knowing how to utilize the grace of God and to constantly acquire deeper degrees of love and faith—in other words, learn the art of taking the pound that is given them by an instantaneous work of grace and trading with that pound so as to be constantly increasing in the wealth of the Holy Spirit—they will find their religous wealth will evanesce, just as many a rich person who is made rich by a gift, and, not knowing how to handle it, finds his money soon gone.

Let us trace some comparisons between acquiring earthly and heavenly riches:

1. Men who become very rich in money do not stop with simply acquiring enough property for their support, but they want enough to make them independent. Then they find with the increase of riches there comes a strange and fascinating power over their fellows in the world, and so they seek great riches for the sake of the power it gives them in the world.

Now, this same law operates in the hearts of those believers who become very saintly. They discover that simply having enough salvation to get saved into Heaven or for their personal immunity from destruction is a very low standard. When they get an insight into the Scriptures and into the blessed character of God and the enormous provisions for holiness, they see that great faith and vast love gives them a sweep of heavenly power in the moral world. There is a Divine fascination in the possession of holy power with God— power to bless souls— and so they bend their thoughts and powers and talents in acquiring as much grace as possible to make them more useful for God. In both cases there is a thirst for power— one for the earthly life and the other for the spiritual.

2. After the money-making man gets into the full swing of acquiring wealth it soon becomes an all-absorbing passion in his soul. It seizes upon his imagination and sharpens his financial wits; it fills his dreams and turns his entire attention to this one subject, so that other things are gradually excluded from his mind and affections. He often reaches a point where he literally sells himself, soul and body, family and friends, and all his being, to the devil, in order to pile up wealth. He becomes imbued with the one passion— to make money; that is his god, and he is a most passionate devotee.

This same principle works gloriously in high altitudes of the spiritual life, for when a Christian has passed through certain ups and downs, and failures and successes, and crucifixions, and gets, by the mercies of God, into the mighty current of the Divine Spirit where the blessed life of God has been opened up to him, there comes into his life a mighty suction into the will of God. The service of God, out of personal love, becomes a rapidly growing passion in the soul, filling all the mental faculties with pictures of God and grace and Heaven and the coming kingdom. All his affections kindle toward Jesus. He sells himself soul and body to the boundless will of God; he loses interest in all things that do not touch the interests of Jesus; he despises every thing that contravenes his highest holiness and usefulness; he loves his fellows and God's works only as related to God's will and pleasure. The love of God burns like a fire in his breast; his will grows rapidly into more and more conformity to the character and ways of Jesus until, like Christ, the zeal for God eats him up.

3. We are often surprised at the economy of very rich people. We notice that they are more careful in saving the pennies than poor people, and it diverts us to notice how they will instinctively and all the time handle their money as if they were poor. This has grown into the habits of all their life, for this is the way they have acquired and preserved their wealth. This same rule works beautifully in acquiring the riches of God in the soul.

When people get really saintly, so that they mint the heavenly gold of grace, they will be the more careful in all the little matters of grace. They grow sparing in the use of words; they guard their tongues; they spend their spare moments in secret prayer and deep spiritual reading; they watch very thoughtfully for any suggestions from the Holy Ghost, that they may not miss a single telephonic message from the Heavenly Father. They save the little graces, and study to please God in the smallest things, and yet with a gentleness of spirit and sweetness of manner utterly free from scruples and legality. The young or weak Christian cannot understand why these saints should be so thoughtful and diligent in the smallest matters. That is the way they have grown in likeness to Jesus and acquired their heavenly wealth of grace. And they have found, like earth's rich people, that the saving of the heavenly pennies is the way to be rich in God and the way to keep their spiritual wealth.

4. Persons who become millionaires in money are those who have learned to make wealth along one or two special lines of industry or investment, and do not cripple themselves by a multiplicity of enterprises. One man learns thoroughly a certain line of manufacture or investment or trade on land or sea and devotes all his energies to the industry which he most understands. Thousands of men, after having made money, lose it by changing their occupation or investing in some direction where they are not perfectly acquainted. Over one half

the bankruptcies come from this cause—of men branching out into a new industry which they have not learned from the bottom up.

Now, this applies to the spiritual life. There are just as many methods of acquiring great riches and spiritual power as there are methods in money-making. Every soul that reaches deep union with God must learn its own method. If we could have a perfect account of the different modes by which great saints have reached their altitudes of grace we would see a wonderful diversity, and yet a principle of unity, running through them all. When we look at such men as Moses, Job, Elijah, Paul, Lopez, Fenelon, Wesley, and George Muller, and notice the difference in their outward circumstances—some very rich in money, some very poor—notice the difference in their habits of thought, their methods of prayer, their outward ways of serving God, their several crosses, their differences in temptations and trials, and how each learned the method of praying, fighting, suffering, and working with which he became perfectly familiar and could blend it all with God.

Now, if any one of those men had been compelled to have adopted the method of life and study and prayer of any one else it might have been his utter ruin as to holiness or usefulness. And so each soul must learn an individual method of using his trials, his temptations, his weaknesses, his habits of prayer and religious study for himself alone.

Many a Christian has wasted his spiritual life and well nigh ruined his soul by trying to adopt the peculiar methods of some other person. There are many narrow-minded Christians who want other people to adopt their rules of holy living—to eat as they eat, dress as they dress, make the same vows that they make. Instead of understanding that God's life must flow into each soul and take a Divinely natural form in that soul, they fancy that the amount of one's holiness depends upon the outward shape of his physical duties. Learn your own method of grace.

5. After a rich man has struggled through the preliminary stages of acquiring wealth he finds that he can make one hundred thousand dollars a little more easily than he made his first ten thousand. And there come opportunities by which he can, in a few days by a strategic investment, make suddenly great leaps in wealth, because he has learned where wealth lies,

and the demands of the market, and knows how to steer his financial craft through the rapids and take a short cut to the open sea, which an inexperienced business man would never know how to do.

This is true of millionaires in grace. They acquire habits of Divine insight; they see opportunities of great spiritual usefulness; of intercession in prayer; of great victory over some spiritual enemy; of an investment they get in some personal sacrifice that will mount them up one thousand miles higher into the kingdom of God. By a wise stroke of Christ-mindedness, by a season of fasting, by yielding their will oftener to other people, by some self-denial that cuts to the heart, by some lonely, venturesome, misunderstood step of faith, which is regarded as fanatical to other people, they shoot the heavenly rapids, take a short cut into the ocean of God, and acquire suddenly great enlargements in the Holy Spirit. They almost double the power and fulness of their Christian lives and of their rewards in Heaven, because, like the financial expert, they have learned the art of using Divine opportunities.

Business men will sometimes make a venture in business which would frighten a new beginner in finance, but they know how to make the hazard and make a million dollars in a day. The same thing has been done many a time in spiritual wealth by the illuminated saints of God who knew how to launch out by faith in the service of Jesus and sacrifice everything for the glory of God in such steps as frighten weak believers. But after they learn the ways of God they run no risk, for they see a dazzling crown where most professors see only a blank.

6. As men grow in wealth they become serious and deep-thoughted and very simple and quiet in their life and manners. As a rule people of very small fortunes are those who put on airs and are pompous, while those who are very rich seem to have a shyness and seclusiveness which may be produced either from a sense of great responsibilities which wealth brings or from a sense of deep pride and of possessing power over their fellows. Let the cause be what it may, there is a growing quietness and simplicity about them, as if they were weighed down with their wealth. Often times their millions of gold make them afraid and unhappy; and well it may, for most of such rich people are utterly destitute of Jesus and are going into a pauper's eternity and every breath they take brings them

nearer the outer darkness.

Now, this principle acts from opposite causes and in an opposite direction with those who are millionaires in grace. As the soul is loaded with the abiding presence of the Holy Spirit, and the mind is filled with gorgeous visions of God and heavenly things, and the affections are softened, there is a growing thoughtfulness and quietness in the spirit. There is also with it a pathetic burden upon the soul, because every increase of the mind of Christ gives some added sorrow for the world of lost souls, and such Christians grow more simple and of fewer words.

Have you not noticed that new or shallow Christians are the ones who put on airs, and think they must do something extraordinary—that they must act with great noise and zeal and do something to impress the people—just as poor people are the most apt to show their money.

Just as a man can make money until he loses all interest in salvation and actually despises everything pertaining to his soul's interest, so a believer can advance in grace and be filled with God and carried away with the interest of Jesus and His coming kingdom until he despises the riches of earth, because he sees that the honor and the wealth of this earth are the most positive hindrances to his heavenly well-being. If we saw the riches of Christ as we shall one day see them in Heaven, how we would go digging for heavenly gold, and by prayer and study of God's Word lay up treasures in Heaven, where moth and rust will not corrupt and where thieves can never steal it.

CHAPTER 9

WATCHFULNESS

To watch is to look with attention.

There are three kinds of watchfulness— animal, intellectual, and spiritual.

When wild herds are feeding on a prairie one of their number will station himself on the lookout and notify the herd of danger. The watchfulness of dogs and birds and cattle and fishes in the sea has been tabulated long ago in scientific books. The astronomer watches through a telescope with thrilling interest for the transit of a star which occurs only once in a thousand years. This involves many things far above the watch of animals. The Spirit-filled believer watches for the coming of God— in His Word, His providences, or some manifestation of His will— as Moses watched for his commission to go to Egypt, or as Simeon watched for the birth of Jesus, or as the hundred and twenty watched for the tongues of fire.

Watchfulness embraces all the concentrated powers of attention. It is not only the look of the eye, even in physical watching, but of the mind and the affections. To watch is to look thoughtfully either at or for something. Hence religious watchfulness is holy thoughtfulness— a calm, wide awake attentiveness to things spiritual and Divine.

The word "circumspect" means to look all around— to inspect the entire circumference. The living creatures described by Ezekiel were full of eyes, so they could see in every direction. A soul filled with the Holy Ghost is to spread out its thoughtfulness in every direction.

1. Notice the spring of watchfulness, which is the union of love and intellect. To "watch" the way Jesus commanded us, we must have the eye of the mind in the socket of the heart. Unless we love to think on God and on the coming of Jesus and on constant spiritual progress we will never make true Scriptural watchers.

The mother on the seashore watching for the ship that brings her son puts her heart into her eyes. All true watching is of that nature where the desires possess the faculty of attention. Every act that God or any of His creatures perform is never a perfectly true act unless it be the act of love. Every act in the world which is not of love is a false or defective or hypocritical act. Love is the one and only thing in the universe that imparts perfection to any act, for love is the only thing that renders any act easy and beautiful and correct and graceful and appropriate and wise and fruitful and harmonious with God.

Hence a watchful Christian is one whose intellectual faculties are flooded with holy love. He loves to remember the things of God; he loves to stretch his imagination over the vast radiant landscapes of Divine things. He loves to be incessantly choosing the will of God in things great and small; he loves to find God everywhere and in everything. If the love of God is not sufficiently poured abroad in the heart by the Holy Ghost to arouse and inspire the intellectual faculties, the soul will never be a true watcher, but will be stupid and drowsy and sleep at its post at the very time the bright procession of God's mercies are going by.

To hunt for faults is not watchfulness, because it is not the act of love. To be meddlesome, to pry into things that do not contribute to our well-being, to scan people with a cold, critical eye, to be always hunting for heresy, to be alert for invidious comparisons, is the genius of a crooked mind and resembles the wild glare in a maniac's eyes and not the calm, thoughtful gaze of a Heavenly sentinel. Watchfulness, then, is pure love on picket guard.

2. Scriptural watchfulness has three directions to it—upward to God, inward to our spiritual condition, and outward to our environment. It is to watch for God as David did when he said he watched for God in prayer more than they that watch for the morning. It is to look with patient, loving attention for fresh revelations of the character of God, of new openings of His Word, of clear intimation of His will. It is also a devout and intelligent outlook for the fulfillment of prophecy, for occasions of Divine intelligence in the affairs of men. It is to keep the telescope of holy vigilance sweeping the heavens of God's grace and providence like the wise men who were on the lookout for the star of Bethlehem. It has been said, "He that notes a special

providence will never lack a special providence to note." It is wonderful how people find what they look for, and holy watchfulness toward God will find Him where foolish indifference sees only blank space.

A watchful Christian will keep guard over his own inner spirit; he will notice the uprising of every disposition, of the trend of his thoughts, and of the choice of his will, and of his words, and the tones of his voice, and of his manners. He will not only watch his actions, but under the swift and beautiful guidance of the Holy Spirit he will perceive the very essence and spirit that flows out in the actions and words. This is what the Lord means by saying, "Keep thy heart with all diligence, for out of it are the issues of life."

Holy vigilance must also guard our environment and be on the lookout for the approaches of Satan in multiplied forms, and keep on the alert for escaping all evil, and doing all the good we can, to see and seize the golden opportunities that an infinite providence brings to us. This is the range of a Bible sentinel. It may seem like a tiresome task, but if the soul is flooded with Divine love it will not only be easy but a chosen occupation of the chastened and sanctified intellect.

3. The condition for watchfulness is that of great quietness of spirit. Flurry of heart, agitation of spirit, or gloomy, despondent foreboding, or terrified feelings of alarm, or a fatigued spirit of legalism that drags itself in the service of God, all unfit a soul for watchfulness.

True watchfulness implies the concentration of all the faculties, and a sentinel must watch with his ears and the sense of smell as well as his eyes. To watch well we need light to see and stillness to hear. It is against the law to talk to the motorman on an electric car, or an engineer on a fast train, or the man on the lookout of a steamship at sea.

God's watchers in the darkness of this present age need great stillness of spirit, or they will fail to see the things they are appointed to observe. Many Christians are so filled with bustle, and noise, and hurry, and excitement, and fret, and criticism, and scheming, and everlasting talkativeness, they cannot detect the gentle tick of God's telegraphic messages, or the soft cooing of the Heavenly dove, or the footsteps of the coming King, and neither can they know what is going on in their own hearts.

I remember once I was praying one Sabbath morning with

a congregation. I was just about uttering a certain word in prayer, but as I was in a recollected state of mind quick as thought the Holy Spirit flashed into my mind that such a word might sound severe or inappropriate. He gave me another word, and prompted me to slightly drop and soften the tone of my voice as I led the prayer. Almost immediately I felt a strong sense of God's presence, and when the "amen" was said and the congregation arose, I found scores of people had been melted to tears during the prayer. I learned from this that if we were still in our hearts before God, and our minds were in a thoughtful, recollected state, it was the most favorable condition for receiving gentle intimations from God, and also the best condition for being channels of grace to others.

4. Watchfulness is to become a heavenly habit of the mind. It is not an instantaneous blessing, like pardon or cleansing, but an habitual attitude of the mind which we must choose and cultivate. It is a sort of human omniscience and corresponds in the creature with the attribute of foreknowledge in God. It is that state of the spiritual understanding referred to by Paul in Philippians, where he prays that the love of God may so abound in us that our knowledge and judgment and mental senses may be flooded with holy love that we may be able to discriminate the things that are excellent. It is to have a mind soaked in Divine grace.

This habit of heavenly watchfulness is the attitude of the soul for meeting Jesus when He comes. It is to a real watchful believer that Christ reveals the things concerning His second coming and millennial reign. It is watchfulness of spirit that fills its vessel with oil, and trims its lamp, and keeps ready for that long expected but swiftly hastening hour, when the cry shall ring through the earth, "Behold the Bridegroom cometh, go ye forth to meet Him."

Watchfulness is the grandest of all holy works, and resembles the work of God in that it accomplishes the greatest results with the least notice.

CHAPTER 10

DANGERS TO DEEP SPIRITUALITY

The very thought of being on probation involves the idea of danger.

In a fallen world like this, there can be nothing good that does not have its special enemy. The closer a soul lives to God, the more subtle are the dangers and difficulties to be overcome. To help those who are seeking to live a life of constant prayer and fellowship with God, we may notice some of the points of danger to a spiritual life.

1. The danger of the soul getting in bondage to its own religion. In passing through a crisis of great crucifixion, and yielding up to God, the mind is apt to get directed to some human measurements of sanctity, or the imitating of some other good person, and under the tension of the hour make rash vows which are afterwards found impracticable, or too severe, or unscriptural. Some souls are specially liable to the danger of scruples, and nothing in the world will more completely cripple a soul than to be in bondage to scruples. It is the policy of Satan to get conscientious people to put scrupulosity in the place of a good conscience.

There is a world of difference between a good conscience enlightened by Scripture, and a fictitious conscience which is in constant dread of a thousand imaginary sins. A scrupulous person torments himself by asking, shall I eat this or that kind of food today, shall I wear this or that suit of clothes today, shall I take this or that train, shall I make a fire on Sunday to keep warm, and a thousand such questions which the Word of God does not teach upon, and is left by Providence to the realm of common sense.

One of the most holy men I ever knew was in great bondage to scruples. In going to preach one Sabbath, he had to cross a river on a ferry boat. His soul was full of joy, but after crossing the river an evil spirit whispered, "You have lost your sanctification by crossing on a steam boat." Instantly his joy was gone, his face was downcast, and he went to church, confessed himself a backslider, and went to the altar for prayers. The whole thing was a trick of Satan.

If a soul begins to get in bondage to its own holiness, there is no telling to what foolish extreme their scruples will carry them. Sometimes persons make a definite profession of heart purity, and really have the experience, but afterwards lose the grace, and yet they feel they must still cling to their testimony, for they think it would ruin things and hurt the cause of God to admit their loss of grace, and so they are in bondage to their confession. Hence, through a false conscience, some will confess they have lost all religion when they have done nothing wrong, and others who have actually lost grace refuse to confess it through a scrupulous fear of hurting the cause of God. Thus from the same root of a false conscience there will come opposite effects. Others make rash vows about eating, or drinking, or clothing, or the marriage relation, or riding on Sunday, or fasting, or the use or non use of medical remedies, and make these vows a sort of imaginary Divinity. They get themselves tangled up into a thousand difficulties, until their spiritual life is a long drawn torment, instead of being that restful, peaceful walk with God in the liberty of perfect love.

Be careful that your own holiness does not become a slave master. I knew a man who gave his tenth to God, and vowed he would never borrow any of the Lord's tenth. But he secretly prided himself on keeping that financial vow, and then the Lord got him into such a strait that he was compelled to break the vow, and borrow the Lord's tenth to buy coal with or freeze. It cured him of depending on his own holiness. If a saint depends on his own religion, God will find a way to smash the idol. God wants us to love Him instead of loving our own vows or our holiness.

2. Another danger to deep piety is that spirit of exclusiveness, seceding from other good people, forming close corporations, thinking that we cannot worship to much profit with other Christians. This is a temptation to spiritual people in every age, but when they get into deeper union with God, and their whole hearts are dissolved in love, they have an ocean-like sympathy for those who are in any and every degree of grace.

It is true that deeply spiritual people find special help and a heavenly delight most in those who are closest to God. And I do not refer to that Divine arrangement by which spiritual people instinctively seek fellowship with kindred minds, for this is an unchanging law of character in Heaven and earth. But I refer to the terrible snare of spiritual pride, of seceding from good people, and holding clandestine meetings, and fancying that they constitute a peculiar aristocracy, which shuts them off from the broad fellowship of good people. In every such instance, spiritual pride soon runs to seed and brings its doctrines either to open disgrace or to a sort of insane nonentity. Numerous instances could be cited.

Avoid any religion that takes on a clandestine form, that works in a dark room, and that puts on the ostentatious wisdom of the owl. We must seek to be very simple, humble, open, frank; and while we have Divine secrets, we carry them as the sunshine carries its seven colors, concealed in the heart while living in the open day.

3. Another danger to deep religion is that of wanting to take leadership. If a soul is useful, it must in some sense be a leader of other souls. People who at one time are so humble that it is a cross to take leadership in anything often, when they once get in the traces and accustomed to being at the front in meetings or Christian work of any kind, after a while there springs up imperceptibly in the heart a thought of assuming leadership in some form or other.

It is true God does raise up people to be leaders in every line of His work, and He especially qualifies persons for such responsibilities. But when a soul forms any desire for leadership, it becomes a poison in the heart. If God uses a Christian in an evangelistic work, or literary work, or mission work, after a while there comes the thought of leadership. This thought is revolved in the mind, then the affections take hold on the thought, until there accumulates a strong desire for leadership. By and by the will begins to act and plan and pull wires and manage things with reference to leadership. The next step is to get certain people and things out of the way that hinder this leadership, and when that is accomplished then there comes a self-complacency of position, and a secret joy in the exercise of authority. Then there comes next a spirit of proscription, cutting off everybody that infringes on this authority, and a jealousy of rulership. And then at last it ripens into religious tyranny and popery, dictating to those who are under it, forbidding them to hear anyone else preach or to have any individual liberty. Then there comes the frown of God on such a leader, and on his or her enterprize, then a disruption, and a collapse, and people stand off and wonder why such and such religious leaders should seem failures, especially when they used to be so useful.

This is the history of spiritual ambition, and this is what it comes to. The only person fit to be a spiritual leader is one whose heart is not in the least set upon it, and who fills the place of leadership with a meek spirit, utterly free from jealousies or envy, and who secretly trembles with every additional power conferred upon him. It does not depend on the size of the enterprize, whether it be a prayer meeting, or Bible class, or camp meeting, or a great mission movement, or a church organization, the spirit is the same. If we walk with God, we must put from us every infinitesimal desire of wanting to be a leader, and if God thrusts it upon us, take it with fear and trembling, and be glad at any time to give it up. This is to keep where there is none of self but all of Christ.

4. Another fruit of spiritual danger is that of religious legality. There are souls who are too eager about growing in grace, they want to be extra good. Somehow they feel that the plain, old-fashioned holiness of simply loving God with all their heart is not enough for it, and so they are inclined to take on things that will indicate a higher religion. Such souls are open to a whole pack of Satan's hounds. They soon run back into Judaism and load themselves down with the laws of the old Jews, supposing it a proof of superior holiness. They feel they must keep the Jewish Sabbath, and conform to circumcision, and observe new moons, and get tangled up with a score of technicalities, and by and by they drift into annihilation, second probation, and all sorts of delusions, and all because they never believed in their hearts that perfect love was the fulfilling of the law.

St. Paul had a world of trouble with such people. He says they began in the spirit and then thought they had to go back to the Jewish law to be made perfect. And when they got in bondage to new moons, and Sabbath days, and various baptisms, and in bondage to their food, and their clothing, he said he was afraid of them, lest all his work for them should be fruitless. There are hundreds of just such poor, silly sheep today, who think they must jump out of the clover fields of pure, boundless love to God and their fellows, and get into the briar patch of outward legalism, in order to show off their extra piety. But they invariably lose their sweet peace and become argumentative, and get distressed in their minds, confused in their faith, and wear a haggard look in their faces. Beware of legalism in holiness.

5. Another danger in the spiritual life is the giving or receiving of personal praise. I do not mean a proper expression of appreciation and holy Christian love. But every grace has an opposite vice, just as every substance has its shadow. The giving of personal praise, which is very apt to be tinctured with flattery, is a danger to the one who gives it. But it is ten times more dangerous to receive praise from others. I am not denying the legitimate facts of Christian character and self-consciousness. A good man who loves and obeys God is just as conscious of his integrity as he is of his existence, and the old teaching that a pure-hearted person must all the time be attributing wicked things to himself is utterly false and unscriptural. But while a soul may be conscious of inward purity and that it is living for the glory of God, yet if such a soul receives praise into the heart it becomes poison in the fountains of love.

The danger lies, as it always does, right at that delicate point where the affections begin to take hold of the praise. If we are well spoken of, or our talents, or our work, or our piety is lauded, and we have the least sensation of being inwardly tickled, or elated, or pleased with such laudation, it becomes a snare at once, and the next thing will likely be a terrible humiliation. If ever we are praised, either for our character, or gifts, or work, it should cause us to instinctively shrink back with a secret trembling in our souls, and a desire to creep off in some quiet place where we can pray to God and realize our unworthiness more deeply than ever.

The holy man who walks constantly with God is one who merits great honor and reward, and yet shrinks from it, and in his heart is pained with all laudation of himself. Thousands of Christians have been well nigh ruined in their inner lives, not because they were praised, but because they sipped it as a sweet wine and allowed their affections to drink it in, and the intoxication proved a curse. Wesley wrote to Asbury that he "studied to be small." No wonder the Lord could so use him. A universe of praise would hurt no one if they did not receive it into their affections and take a measure of joy in it, just as a diver can descend in the ocean with perfect safety as long as the ocean is kept outside of him.

To please God we must constantly, as a thoughtful, fixed habit of the soul, seek only the honor that comes from Him. How many times have we seen a young preacher or Christian worker get puffed up with a little praise. But remember that the same danger runs up into the altitude of Christian experience, and the very worst form of spiritual pride is to take into the heart the praise for personal piety. Even when we are flooded with Divine joy, the Holy Ghost tells us to "rejoice with trembling." There is a beautiful holy fear which the very holiest soul needs, and the God that inhabits eternity tells us that He fixes His eye especially on that kind of holiness that in self-abasement "trembles at His Word."

6. To walk in the Holy Spirit we must discern and repudiate what is called touchiness, that is, feeling miffed and hurt because we are corrected, or advised, or warned of some danger by other people. People who profess holiness and yet fancy they are beyond being taught, or above being reproved for their mistakes or imprudent conduct, and are not willing to be advised by solid Christians, will soon find themselves ground to powder by the millstones of God's providence.

In every single gathering of Christians there will be found those who seem to be very bright in religion, and yet who are utterly unwilling to listen to sober counsel, and who show that they are vexed or sullen if older and wiser Christians in the least reprove them for a blunder. Such persons need revelation from God as to the correct nature of holiness. Self-conceit seems to be a special malady attending religious experiences; but, mark you, the self-conceit does not come from grace, but lies in the nature of the mind. Hot sunshine makes the snake to crawl, but snakes are a very different thing from poor sunshine. Warm degrees of grace seem to evoke certain latent infirmities of the mind.

To be deeply spiritual we need to avoid the very semblance of touchiness and self-opinionatedness. The only cure for getting miffed and having our feelings hurt, and being moody, and sullen, or tart, and curt in our words, is to be utterly dissolved in Divine charity, where we love God and everybody with such a sweet and impartial spirit that we care nothing for our own feelings and can receive advice and reproof from others in real humility and thankfulness.

There are other dangers that beset the pathway of the soul as it journeys up the mountains of grace, but if we can constantly avoid the foregoing evils it will rapidly facilitate our conformity to the image of Jesus.

CHAPTER 11

The Practice Of God's Presence

Nearly everything in the Christian life depends upon our views of God, the conceptions we form of Him, the standpoints from which we view Him, and the different relationships we apprehend that He sustains to us.

There is a difference between a moral life and a spiritual life. A moral life has its eye on duty and depends upon our views of law. But a spiritual life has its eye on the life of God and can be produced only by faith; and faith is the soul's vision of God. There are many types of piety, and these various types of the Christian life are moulded by our views of God. Of all the millions of professed Christians, only a small percent reach that state of life where the mind is habitually stayed on God. And yet we never get into the very heart of religion, or into a true Scriptural life, until God becomes the paramount abiding and ever increasing attraction of the mind, so that He habitually fills our meditations; and if the attention should be diverted for a while by pressure of other interests, as quick as it is liberated it flies back like the needle to the pole, with a sweet thirst to repose on God and to lovingly search into His ways and adjust itself to His presence.

A spiritual mind is an intellect that has become throughly spiritualized by the Divinely infused habits of the Holy Spirit, and where the understanding has been, as it were, turned into a heart, and is an instrument of Divine love, instead of being a mere instrument of cold human reason.

A spiritual mind is an intelligence set on fire with God's love. To be spiritually minded, the Holy Ghost tells us, is life and peace. Now it is the spiritual mind that practices the presence of God. And yet there are numberless degrees to this holy activity of the soul. And also, there are various forms in which a devoted soul may habitually look upon God. All these various forms of contemplating God are true and Scriptural, but some of them are more powerful and fruitful than others. Our special type of spiritual character will be fashioned by what is our dominant view of God.

1. Among our earliest views of God is that of picturing Him as sitting on the throne of the universe in the Heaven of heavens, surrounded by myriads of angels and saints, and manifesting Himself to the heavenly host in forms of dazzling splendor which no unglorified eye could possibly look upon. This is the picture given to us in several places in Scripture and one that every human being needs to form clearly in his mind. (See I Kings 22:19; Revelation 8:2-5). This is the thought that comes to us as children, and as beginners in the spiritual life, from the unfolding of those words, "Our Father who art in Heaven."

This habitual view of God greatly aids us in the conception of His majesty and the excessive glory of His court, and develops the thought of His authority and administration over all worlds and creatures, sending forth His messengers with lightning speed into all parts of the universe, and receiving the homage and melodious praise of myriads on myriads of holy angels and saints. Now while this is a true and essential view of God, it does not embrace all the truth. And if we should make it our predominant view of God it would not produce the highest fruits of spiritual living, for there is a far awayness in it that admits of too much space between God and the daily habits of the soul, somewhat similar to those enormous stars which are fifty times bigger than our sun, and yet their great distance weakens their action upon our planet as well as their impression upon our minds.

2. The next mode of apprehending God as a habit of spiritual meditation is that of looking upon Him in His external immensity, as filling all space and all eternity, like an infinite atmosphere enveloping all worlds, an invisible, inaudible, inscrutable substance of spirit, forever reposing in a motionless calm; moving all things, yet Himself unmoved; seeing all things, yet Himself unseen; knowing all things, yet Himself unknown; upholding all things, yet Himself needing no upholding; with an infinite personality in every point of space and every moment of duration, living in one eternal now, whose center is everywhere and whose circumference cannot be found.

This view of God is also true and Scriptural, as we find

stated in the 139th Psalm and many other passages. This is the view of God especially congenial to philosophical minds and persons of extensive imaginations. There are great benefits to be derived from the frequent exercise of stretching our thoughts out as far as possible over the immensity of God, and frequently contemplating with holy awe the eternity of His existence. It lifts the mind up above the littleness of the earth and time. It reveals to us the emptiness of a thousand things that otherwise seem great and solid. Perhaps no one can reach a state of walking with God in daily contemplation without forming these views of the loftiness and immensity of God.

3. The next stage in the practice of God's presence is the habit of contemplating Him more particularly in His relation to us personally. It is that conception of Him as a pure, Divine presence, enveloping us round and enclosing us every moment with all His blessed attributes, like a transparent sea, walling us in and bathing us evermore with the placid wave of His will and knowledge and love. When this view of God is properly formed it gives us a more realizing sense of His personal relationship to us, and it makes us apprehend more clearly His various attributes until we almost feel the play of those attributes upon us like Divinely delicate fingers that incessantly hold us up.

In this contemplation of God we see it is His power that preserves us, and our feet do not walk on the earth so much as it is that we are stepping on the omnipotent, outspread hand of God, and our heads are canopied with His protection, and our bodies are surrounded with His arm. It is His wisdom that fashions and superintends the intricate machinery of our being. It is His life that each successive instant supplies all the vitality to our bodies, minds, and spirits. It is His knowledge that never for a second forgets or omits anything connected with our well-being. It is His grace that continually prompts us in all the life of faith. Thus in whatever way we view His surrounding presence we get a glimpse of His magnificent attributes in their action upon us.

4. But all these ways of looking at God, in which we seem to be bringing His blessed presence closer and closer to us, will not accomplish the highest results of a life of true holiness until we view the personality and presence of God as invading the very center of our being and enthroning Himself within us.

It is a day to date from when the Holy Spirit flashes the beautiful light all through our minds that God Himself, the eternal and living God in three persons, as Father, Son, and Comforter, have enthroned themselves in the depths of our inner nature. This light is flashed into different minds in different ways, and often in different ways in successive periods to the same person. Sometimes it seems like the form of a white dove softly brooding in the breast, and sometimes like a bubbling fountain of sweet, transparent water gushing up in the heart, and sometimes like a soft, whispering voice speaking in the soul. Sometimes it seems like a Divine man that glides into us and stands erect in our inner being, filling every limb and feature with Himself, and sometimes like a hot, sweet furnace that quivers, and glows, and melts us into unspeakable love and tears. And in some rare instances it seems like the indescribable presence of three Divine persons that sit serenely in the soul and hush the whole being into adorable awe.

It is this contemplation of God that brings His royal court, as it were, down from the third heavens and locates it in our souls, in which the heart becomes His throne and the conscience the organ of His legislation, and the will the glad executive of His purpose. It is this view of God dwelling in us that is the highest and most fruitful, and the view which is especially presented in the New Testament where Jesus says, "The Spirit will flow out of you like rivers of waters;" and again, "The Comforter will abide in you;" and again, "My Father will love him, and we will come and make our abode with him." And again, "I will dwell in them and walk in them;" and again, "It is not I that live, but Christ liveth in me."

It is this view of God that repeats over again the Divine mystery of the incarnation, and the soul seems to be another Mary, carrying its adorable Lord and being steeped in thought and feeling from His indwelling presence.

Now it is worthy of notice that this form of God's presence, as filling us with all His personality and glorious character, is the very thing that the Holy Spirit makes a devout soul to hunger for. We never hear any Christian expressing a great desire to be enveloped in God, but they do have that sweetly distressing thirst to have all their inner nature flooded with the living God. The Holy Spirit begets within us those prayers and forms of spiritual thirst which are according to God's words and the Father's will.

Now we are not to neglect the other views of God, as enthroned in the heavens, or as expanded through all the universe and residing intimately in every atom of creation, nor that view of Him which presses us round like an outward ocean. They are all true, and the devout mind will carry all these views along with it. But we are to emphasize that habitual view of God as living within us, making us a miniature center of His blessed government, revealing Himself to our inner spiritual senses, and uniting us to Himself in a Divine union of nature, character, love, and service, by which He makes us the vessels of His gracious presence, in order that we may afterwards be vessels of His glorious presence.

It is this practice of God's presence that sinks us into deep humility, that weans and quiets all our faculties, and that makes us the docile agents of His will.

There are many degrees of these spiritual habits, and if any one is not yet familiar with this spiritual practice let him not be discouraged, but with patient perseverance keep the mind on God in humble prayer that He shall powerfully reveal Himself in the inner life as an abiding presence.

CHAPTER 12

The Saint's Dressing Room

A beautiful picture of the steps and degrees of salvation is sketched by St. Paul in Colossians 3:1-14.

It is a picture of believers looking for the return and personal appearing of Christ and preparing to meet Him, by putting off the old sinful garments, and dressing themselves up in the pure white raiment of spiritual graces, to be ready to meet Him.

He says that our life is now "hidden with Christ in God," but that "Christ is going to appear again," that is, visibly come back to the earth, and that when He thus "appears," "we will also appear with Him in glory." Now for this cause we are to "put to death" every sinful disposition, and put off our natural sinful clothing, and put on the graces of Christ, as His Bride, to be ready for the wedding.

The passage may be called the saints' dressing room. The word "put" occurs five times in these verses— two puttings off, and three puttings on. This itself is suggestive of the difference between sin and salvation, that grace is larger than sin. God makes the plaster larger than the sore for "where sin abounded, grace does much more abound." There is a limit to sin, but there is no limit to the things of God. Also there is a limit and a completion to forgiving and cleansing away sin, so that it can be finished; but there is no limit to growth in the knowledge and love of God.

1. We are to "put off" all actual sin, the committing of sin, and the purpose and intent of committing sin. Verse 8, "Put off all these: anger, wrath, malice, blasphemy, filthy conversation, and telling lies." The apostle does not mention every kind of actual sin in this list, but he does mention sin of every class, which implies the whole catalogue. Every sin that is committed comes under one of three heads, as earthly, or sensual, or devilish. Now the sins mentioned by Paul cover all of these heads.

In order to be justified we must renounce all these sins and lay ourselves perfectly helpless and lost in the hands of Jesus, depending alone upon His merit and the substitution of His death for us.

2. "Put off the old man with his deeds." This second "put" refers to our giving up of original sin, or the old self life. Our natural depravity is spoken of in Scripture under several names, such as "the carnal mind," "unrighteousness," "the body of sin," "an evil heart," "the old man," and other terms. It is called "the old man," because it is the essence and image of Adam. It is that principle of self life which has all the traits of Adam. Like Adam it shuns contact with intense holiness, and then tries to hide itself under the fig leaves of human righteousness, and then lays the blame of its downfall on some one else.

We may be young, but we all have "an old man" which has descended through the human race for six thousand years. This carnal self-life is found in every human heart. It is deeper than actual sin, for it is in the infant before he commits sin, and remains in the believer after all his own sins have been pardoned. It is not to be repressed, but "put off" by the perfect consecration to God's will, which places the soul where the Holy Spirit can sanctify the heart.

3. "Put on the new man, which is renewed in knowledge after the image of Christ." This third "put" refers to the work of heart purity. The image of Christ is a human heart from which all sin has been purged, and which Christ occupies by His Spirit. Our Lord had a perfect human nature, with all the functions, appetites, affections, and capabilities of a human being, as man was first created. He had no sin in any part of His compound being. The apostle says, "He was made in the likeness of sinful flesh," but He had no sinful flesh.

Now to put on the image of Christ is to receive Jesus as our Sanctifier and let Him, through the working of the Holy Ghost, come into us and take the exact place that the "old man" occupied before. Thus the pure, living Christ becomes to us, and in us, just what the old self and the old Adam used to be, the fountain from which flows all the streams of actual living.

The apostle goes on to say that when "we put on the new man," we get into a condition "where there is neither Greek, nor Jew, Barbarian, Scythian, bond nor free, but Christ is all and in everything." The principle of caste is a terrible proof and manifestation of the "old man" in the heart. In Eastern countries every person is bound by inflexible customs of caste, and it is the source of countless and heartless cruelties, ignorance, and crimes of every sort. In so-called civilized countries it still operates with great power between the classes of rich and poor, of nobility and peasantry, and between different nationalities and different sections of the same country. Even the visible Church is sliced up into factions by this Damascus blade of caste.

There never has been, and never will be, any true unity of heart among human beings except on the basis of a pure heart, full of Divine love. When we put on the second Man from Heaven, when Christ becomes in us an actual power what the "old man" used to be, then we rise into a new spiritual race, with a new head, and under the sway of a new love, where the divisions and strifes between nations, and races, and classes, cease to exist.

4. Put on the virtues of Christ. Just exactly as all the vices flow out from the "old man," until they cover the life, so all the graces flow out from the living Christ, until the whole life is covered over with them. Hence the connection between this verse and the previous one. "Put on therefore, as the elect of God, holy and beloved, bowels of mercies, kindness, humbleness of mind, meekness, longsuffering; forbearing one another, and forgiving one another." Here are seven virtues, the perfect number of the Christ life; and all these graces are to sprout out from the living Christ and spread themselves over our souls and lives, as the leaves of a vine spread themselves over an arbor.

Every living thing grows for itself a garment out of its own life. A sheep grows a garment of wool, a hog a garment of bristles, a fish of scales, a bird of feathers, a tree a garment of leaves, the "old man" a garment of all sorts of vices, and the Christ life grows a pure raiment of the seven graces which are here specified. And yet we are commanded to put these graces upon us. We are to do this by persistently and believingly receiving Christ to take the place in us that inbred sin had. We are to choose and appropriate all these graces and cooperate with the Holy Spirit in making them our daily habit and our very life. When the heart comes forth from the bath of the cleansing blood of Jesus, it is then to be clothed with all the virtues of Christ through the operation of the Holy Ghost.

"As the elect of God." No word in Scripture is more utterly misunderstood than this word "elect." It is always used in the Bible in connection with sanctification, or of being a Bridehood saint, or in connection with a certain "rank" among the saved ones. There is not a single instance in the New Testament where the word elect is ever used in connection with the conversion or the new birth. "We are elect through sanctification." "We are to make our calling—which really means our conversion, and our election—which refers to our sanctification, both sure." In this passage the apostle is urging believers to get ready to meet Christ as His Bride, "when He shall appear." And having put off actual sin, and then put off the "old man," and then put on the new man, the living person of Christ in the heart, he then speaks of them as being holy and being the "elect." Now they are to dress themselves in gracious garments, fit for their rank.

"Bowels of mercies." This is the first undergarment that the Bride of Christ puts on her pure heart. It is a disposition of great tenderness, compassion, and sympathy. It is a softness of heart for all who are lost, and fallen, and degraded, and a deep yearning over them which is the first virtue that belongs to the Incarnation, when Jesus came down from the Father to save the lost.

Had I the space, I could show that every virtue, under intense feeling, acts upon a certain part of the mind, or the body; as love on the physical heart, anger on the eye, thought on the brain, and compassion and grief on the bowels. There is a deep scientific reason for every word in Scripture, and a Divine reason for saying "bowels of mercies."

"Kindness." This is a slight change of the word "kin-ness," that is, the feeling of peculiar regard we have for those who are our family kin—the mutual feelings of those of the same kind or the same species. There is a universal law by which creatures of the same kind herd together, feel for each other, and love each other. This law runs up into the spiritual world. More than this, this feeling of peculiar fellowship becomes stronger as we enter into certain mental and moral states with other souls. Just as mentally a poet feels his kinship with other poets, so spiritually the saints feel their kinship with other saints in the same proportion that they enter into the trials, the faith, the experiences of those saints.

I was once reading about Abraham in the Bible and suddenly it opened up to my heart that he was a very near and dear relative of mine. And in a flash of light and love I seemed to get a thorough understanding of his life of faith, and he seemed a personal acquaintance. The Bible characters are God's chosen vessels of revealing different species of character. We never know Job till we go through something of what he went through. The higher critics, who deny the personality and real life of Job, advertise themselves as only philosophical animals, who never entered Job's species or kind. Divine kindness is to extend to everybody that thoughtful love that God extends to the human race.

"Humbleness of mind." A humility that is willing to learn, to be reproved, to be corrected, to confess its mistakes, to make no display of its gifts. A humility that knows without boasting of its knowledge. It takes a marvelous depth of crucifixion to kill mental pride and put on humbleness of mind.

"Meekness." That is, humility before God. Self-abasement, self-depreciation, self-distrust. The not contending for our rights, or our honor, or our reputation, but leaving it all with God.

"Longsuffering." That is, suffering patiently just as long as God may see fit for us to suffer. The not putting any limit to our trials or crosses, and never saying, "I will not endure this any longer." It is an unlimited abandonment of ourselves to Jesus, for better or worse, for suffering or joy.

"Forbearing one another." The mutual and loving endurance with each other's faults. We are each in many ways a cross to one another, and no amount of holiness can possibly prevent us, in this life, from being a cross or a care to someone else. It takes two bears to keep house, namely "bear and forbear."

"Forgiving one another." The having a heart full of a forgiving spirit, so as to be prone to forgive, to prefer forgiving people than to harbor a feeling of hardness or harshness toward anyone.

These are the seven beautiful, soft, silken, spotless undergarments that "the elect" souls are to put on by the power of the Holy Ghost, working out from the very life of Christ. As the warm spring sun shines on the grape vine, and brings out the beautiful green garniture of leaves, covering the vine and trellis; so the warm shining of the Holy Ghost upon the true Christ vine planted in the heart brings forth the sweet foliage of these seven graces to cover the life of the perfect believer.

5. "Above all these things put on charity," that is, Divine love, which is the "bond of perfectness." In Eastern countries the outer garment, in full dress, as a rule, is a pure white mantle. The elect soul that is preparing to meet the Heavenly Bridegroom is to put on over all the graces, that overflow of Divine love that covers the whole being and is the pledge, the proof of Scriptural perfection.

There is a maturity in grace, where the soul is melted with the love of God, and glows and burns with universal charity, and, like a river overflowing its banks, inundates all the country around. It is this outer garment, with its long flowing skirts of charity, that prepares us to sit down at the wedding supper when the King appears.

CHAPTER 13

Eating the Book

There are several passages in the Bible which speak of "eating the Words of God," and of "eating the Book," and of "man not living by bread alone but by every word that proceedeth out of the mouth of God." Let us put together some of these verses.

"Thy words were found, and I did eat them, and Thy word was unto me the joy and rejoicing of mine heart. . . . I sat alone because of Thy hand, for Thou hast filled me with indignation" (Jer. 15:16,17). "But Thou, Son of Man. . . open Thy mouth, and eat that I give thee. And when I looked, behold, an hand was sent unto me; and, lo, a roll of a book. . . written within and without with lamentations, and mourning, and woe" (Ezek. 2:8-10). "So I opened my mouth, and He caused me to eat that roll. And He said unto me, Son of Man. . . fill thy bowels with this roll that I give thee. Then did I eat it; and it was in my mouth as honey for sweetness. . . . So the Spirit lifted me up and took me away and I went in bitterness" (Ezek. 3:2,3,14). "And the voice said, Go and take the little book which is open in the hand of the angel. . . . And I went unto the angel, and said unto him, give me the little book. And He said unto me, Take it, and eat it up; and it shall make thy belly bitter, but it shall be in thy mouth sweet as honey" (Rev. 10:8,9).

All of these passages agree in the following points: that the Word of God can be eaten; that it is sweet to the taste; and that afterward there is sorrow and anguish of spirit corresponding to the taste of bitterness. Before we examine minutely into these three facts let us preface the thought that all these passages refer especially to God's Word entering the soul of one who is called to be a prophet, or teacher, or Gospel preacher; and while, in a modified degree, these truths apply to all Christians, yet in a special way they apply to those who are the messengers of salvation. Now let us notice thoughtfully the following points.

1. It is a spiritual reality that the Word of God can be eaten by the human soul under the operation of the Holy Spirit. The teachings of Scripture are so often called a mere metaphor, and spiritual facts have been so much relegated to poetry and mysticism, until very few Bible readers apprehend the reality of the inspired Word. It is not a mere figure or poetical emblem to say that we can eat the Word of the Lord.

A spiritual fact is just as much a fact as a material one, and because the Word of God is a spiritual force, and because the eating of it by the human heart is a spiritual act, that does not render it any the less a fact than the taking of material food into the mouth. The same God who produces material bread for man's body produces the inspired words of Scripture for man's spiritual nature. And these words, which proceed out of God's mouth, are just as literally the life and nourishment of man's soul as the created wheat and corn furnish nourishment for the body. Furthermore, just as far as man's spiritual being is superior to his fleshly body, so God's words are superior to all the material creation. Jesus Himself affirms this when He says that "Heaven and earth shall pass away, but My words shall not pass away."

God's material creation lies outside of the Divine nature and is not united to His eternal personality. But God's words are expressions of the attributes and qualities of God's person and character. Hence His words are loaded with a vitality, sweetness, richness, persistency, and energy infinitely above the atoms or laws of the material world.

The life of God's words does not lie in the mere letters, or language, or sound of those words, but in their absolute truthfulness, and that truthfulness constitutes their spiritual force and nourishment. God's Word is the expression of His thought for our mind, of His love for our heart, of His sovereignty for our will, of His justice for our conscience, of His Providence for our need, of His wrath for our sins, of His grace for our salvation, of His sweetness for our comfort, of His eternal beauty for our imagination, of His glory for our elevation, and of His threefold personality for our communion and everlasting fellowship.

Thus every truth in God as uttered in His Word corresponds with the capabilities and the needs in our nature. And when those words are received by our understanding, and appropriating faith, they become grafted into our spiritual being and form our life and nourishment. The vital force of God's words may even sustain the body, without physical hunger, whenever it pleases the Lord to make them perform such a function, as in the case of Moses, Elijah, and Jesus, who went forty days each without eating or drinking, except the sustentation of the Word of the Lord.

2. In all the passages referred to, the first effect of eating the word of God is that it produced a sensation as sweet as honey. Man's spiritual nature has five senses just as really as the body has. And when the Holy Spirit applies Divine truth, or reveals a Divine Person, or unveils vast regions of Heavenly things to the inner man, the inner senses of the soul are just as conscious of these things by spiritual touch, and taste, and vision, and hearing, as the senses of the body recognize the outward things of creation.

God's words are the fragrant blossoms of His pure eternal mind, and it is just as reasonable that when those words enter our spiritual nature, there should be the sensation of sweetness and gladness, as when the odor of flowers enters the sense of smell. Even in our intellectual nature, apart from the operations of grace, when new truth is discovered, or when an old truth is seen in a new relation, there is a thrill of intellectual pleasure. Poets and philosophers have frequently spoken of this as the purest joy possible to man, because they were not acquainted with the higher plane of spiritual joy in the things of God.

Scientists have often been so affected by the discovery of a new star, or some new force in nature, or some outburst of grandeur, or of human eloquence, as to be overcome in their bodily strength and faint away in a similar manner as Christians sometimes lose their physical strength under the manifestation of God's grace and glory to the soul. If the opening to the mind of some new and startling truth, or the listening to the strains of sweet music, or the spell of human eloquence, can so effect people as to make them lose their appetite, or be unconscious of their surroundings, or lose their physical strength, how much more is it possible and reasonable that the unfolding of the words of God to the inner man shall fill and thrill all the inner senses with sweetness, beauty, strength, and Heavenly grandeur to such a degree that the outward bodily frame should be prostrated under the power of Divine manifestation.

The soul is stronger than the body, and the inner spiritual senses, when touched by the Holy Spirit, oftentimes act with such energy that they seem to impart their sensations to the bodily organs. Thus when God speaks to the inner ear, many have felt that His voice was audible. When the Spirit has revealed Jesus to the eye of the heart many have felt that they saw Christ with their fleshly eyes. And when God's words have been Divinely applied to the inner mind, many have felt a sensation of extraordinary sweetness in their mouths.

The Psalmist declares that God's Word was sweeter to his taste than honey, and Jeremiah and Ezekiel affirm the same testimony. The celebrated Marquis De Renty, of France, in the seventeenth century, was so possessed with God's presence that he said when he pronounced the name of God his mouth was filled with a sensation as sweet as honey. The professed Christian scholars who deny these things simply deny them because they have not had the same experience. "The words of Christ are spirit and life," and they can enter our spirits and become our life as literally as food enters our bodies. His words can be tasted as truly as the touch of sweet food.

3. In the next place, all these passages agree in stating that there was a sensation of bitterness, or anguish, or sorrow, that followed as a consequence of eating God's words. But in every instance we notice that this bitterness is mentioned in connection with the ministry of God's Word to rebellious and disobedient people. In other words, eating the Book was delightful to the individual who ate it, but the sensation of bitterness was experienced in connection with ministering the Word to others.

Jeremiah says that eating God's Word was the joy of his heart, but that when he had to take that Word to the assembly of mockers it filled him with pain and indignation. Jer. 15:16-18.

Ezekiel says that eating the roll was like honey in his mouth, but when he had to unroll it to other people who rejected it, it produced lamentation and woe.

St. John tells us that while eating, the Book was sweet in his mouth, but it filled his bowels with bitterness in preaching it to nations and ungodly kings.

These are legitimate Bible experiences which are still transpiring as in all the past. When God calls any one to the true prophetic and apostolic state, it is not for their personal comfort, but that they might enter into the positive fellowship of the crucifixion and ministry of the blessed Jesus, and that is to be a chosen vessel of God's Word to others, whether they will receive or reject it.

To be a chosen messenger of God's pure living Word is the highest office a human soul can fill, but it involves a vast world of interior crucifixion and the breaking down of all human pride, and philosophy, and earthly wisdom, that God's inspired Word may be held in perfect faith and simplicity, unmixed with human creeds, or fleshly sentiment, or popular interpretation. The true prophets of the Lord Jesus must share His sorrows, enter into His feelings, endure His conflicts against Satan and his demons.

The true Holy Ghost preacher identifies himself with God's pure, infallible Word in its plain, literal sense, and shares the fortunes of those words. On the God side they are sweet as honey but outwardly, in relation to Satan and ungodly men and higher critics, there is bitterness and sorrow of heart. But this sorrow is what wins the crown of the true prophet.

CHAPTER 14

THREE KINGDOM STAGES

The only ideal kingdom over creatures is that of a theocracy, where creatures are either mediately or immediately governed by the Lord.

All man-made governments at the best are poor temporary arrangements, and in the end will run into anarchy. A kingdom implies both a king and his subjects.

A perfect king carries all government in himself. There is a significant verse in Isaiah which attributes all the functions of government in its legislative, judicial, and executive departments to the Lord Jesus. "For the Lord is our judge, the Lord is our lawgiver, the Lord is our king; He will save us." And it is worth our notice that these words are a part of a prophecy of Christ's coming reign on the earth. Isaiah 33:22.

A perfect king must have subjects who serve him out of personal love and who have the mind of the king and all the principles of his dominion so inwrought that they need no outward machinery of government, no coercion, but in every one of whose individual souls the king is enthroned as the brightest jewel of their existence, and whose every affection and choice is in union with the king, and who can be governed directly by the king without the agency of intermediate officers. Thus an ideal king carries all his subjects and all his government in his own heart, and ideal subjects carry the king and all his dominion in their hearts, and the government is entirely personal, and not representative or functionary. This ideal king and kingdom is revealed in the Scriptures as being a blessed fruit of redemption, so far as our race is concerned, and as having three great stages in its progress.

The first stage is internal, under the dominion of the personal Holy Ghost.

The next is the outward manifested kingdom, under the personal reign of the Lord Jesus.

The third stage is that of the fixed, eternal state of the revealed and personal dominion of the Father.

In order of the Divine nature, it is first the Father, and then the Son, and then the Holy Ghost; but in the order of forming and establishing the kingdom of God among mankind, it is first the dominion of the Spirit, and then of the Son, and lastly of the Father.

This order of the kingdom is according to grace, for out from the bosom of the Father the Eternal Son came forth to bridge the chasm between a holy God and an unholy world, and by His incarnation and vicarious death and resurrection to save us and make it possible for us to be in the kingdom. Then the glorified Jesus has authority to send forth the Holy Ghost to regenerate and sanctify subjects for the kingdom.

Thus though the Holy Spirit is the last person in the Godhead, He is the missionary person of the Godhead to gather recruits and prepare subjects for the kingdom. And when the missionary offices of Christ and the Holy Ghost are finished, and they have gathered us up from the wreck of sin and anchored us in the placid harbor of the eternal bosom of the Father, then the kingdom will have reached its consummation and everlasting glory. That we may have a more Scriptural vision of these kingdom stages, let us notice them a little in detail.

1. The hidden stage of the kingdom, which is especially under the personal dominion of the Holy Ghost.

The kingdom of God begins in the center of our being, and then spreads itself outwardly from the heart into the mental faculties and the outward life of the senses, motions, and expressions of the body. It is this first stage of the kingdom which is referred to by such Scriptures as, "the kingdom of Heaven is within you," "the kingdom of God is not in word, but in power," "Christ in you, the hope of glory," "your life is hid with Christ in God," "the kingdom of God is not meat and drink, but righteousness, peace, and joy in the Holy Ghost."

This last Scripture is very concise, and is expressive of the three essential departments of any government or kingdom, for "righteousness" is the statutory or legislative power, and "peace," or perfect equity and internal adjustment of harmony, is the judiciary department of the kingdom, and "joy" is the exultant, triumphant, royal grace of the executive office of government.

And as any kingdom must have a law-making, a law-judging, and a law-executing power, these three principles are exactly expressed by righteousness, peace, and joy in the Holy Ghost.

We must not fail to notice this inward kingdom "in the Holy Ghost." It is in connection with this hidden stage of the kingdom which we have in this present life of faith that Jesus gives us a marvelous statement in the fourteenth chapter of John, concerning the indwelling of the three Divine persons. He first says, "If ye love me, and keep my commandments, the Father will give you another Comforter, the Spirit of Truth, to abide with you forever." Then a few verses after, He says, "I will love you, and will manifest myself to you, and will not leave you orphans, but will come to you." And then farther on, He says, "My Father will love you, and we (Father and Son) will come unto you and make our abode with you."

Here are some wonderful steps in the spiritual life, that after we love God we are to receive the personal Holy Ghost, and then have unfolded within us the person and presence of Jesus, and then have manifested to us the adorable person and indwelling of the Father. These matchless promises are to be fulfilled in the present life, and belong to that stage of God's kingdom especially dominated by the Holy Ghost. It is a terrible perversion of Scripture to say that this incoming of the person of Christ in the sanctified heart by the Holy Ghost is the Second Coming of Christ which is promised at the end of the Age. Christ coming to us in the Spirit, and coming to gather us to Himself in the air, are distinguished by the use of different words in the Greek.

The true believer is now living in this world pre-eminently a life of faith, a secret life with God, with a hidden government within Him, with a hidden parliament, a hidden judiciary, and a hidden King. He is a miniature, portable government, unrecognized and unknown by the world, yet with a Divine life of secret royalties and grandeurs that would eclipse all the majesties of the earth if they were made visible.

2. The open, manifested stage of the kingdom, under the immediate and personal sovereignty of the Lord Jesus as the Son of David, the Messiah, the Prince of the kings of the earth.

It betrays great ignorance of Scripture to think that the kingdom of God is never to have any form except that of the hidden dominion of the Holy Ghost. The stage of the open, manifested kingdom of Christ in glory and power on this earth is taught in Scripture a great deal more explicitly and unanimously than even the spiritual kingdom of the heart. To take all such Scriptures only in a mystic or spiritual sense is the greatest blunder of Bible interprepation. Paul tells us expressly in Romans 8 that "creation is waiting in earnest expectation for the manifestation of the sons of God," and that the curse under which creation now groans will then be delivered from bondage into the glorious liberty of the glory of God, proving that the sons of God, who now live a secret life in the Spirit, will at the coming of Jesus be openly manifested in His glorious reign.

Again he tells us in Colossians that we, who now have a hidden life, "when Christ, our life, shall appear, we shall also appear with Him in glory." Again he speaks in his second epistle to Timothy of the "appearing and kingdom of our Lord Jesus," showing that the kingdom is to have an open, visible "appearing" at the personal visible "appearing of Christ."

The angel told Mary that she should bring forth a son, and that God would give Him the throne of His father David, and He should reign over the house of Jacob, and of His kingdom there should be no end. Now if Christ was born of a virgin in literal fact, so His reign on the theocratic throne of David over the twelve tribes of Israel is to be just as literal a fact. And if Christ's reign on this earth is to be only a mystic reign, then His being born of a virgin was only a mystic type, and not literal fact, for the two things are joined together, and both are to be equally literal, visible, and historical.

We are told in Jeremiah 3 that in the last days, when all the tribes of Israel are restored to their own land, "that Jerusalem shall be the throne of the Lord, and all nations shall be gathered unto it, and they shall never again walk after the imaginations of their evil heart."

The living creatures and the elders in Rev. 5, saved from every nation and kindred, magnify Christ as the Lion of the tribe of Judah, and the root of David, and right in connection with it they proclaim that they are kings and priests unto God and shall reign on the earth.

In the parable of the Pounds, Jesus teaches expressly that as soon as He collects a certain number for His kingdom He will return and reign over the very territory that He left when He went into a far country. This is the Church Age, the special dispensation of the Holy Spirit, but the next Age will be more specially the Kingdom Age, under the immediate administration of Jesus. The Holy Spirit will fill the world in the next Age far more than He does now. But notwithstanding that, it will be pre-eminently the Age of the Apocalypse, that is, the unveiling of all hidden things, and the visible manifesting of Jesus and His servants, the stone kingdom which will crush all human governments and fill the world with a theocratic empire. The reign of Christ in His humanity, according to many Scriptures, will extend beyond the millennium "into the generations of the Ages of Ages."

3. The fixed, ultimate, and eternal stage of God's kingdom, which stretches out beyond all known measurements of time, in which all subjects of the kingdom, having been brought into union with the Holy Ghost and the only begotten Son, will be specially under the dominion of the person of the Eternal Father.

The special Scripture on this subject is found in 1 Cor. 15:24-28: "Then cometh the end, when Christ shall have delivered up the kingdom to the Father, when He shall have put down all rule, and authority, and power; then shall the Son Himself be subject unto the Father, that God may be all in all."

This word "end" stretches away into the future, as the words "in the beginning" reach back into the past. Some suppose that this Scripture is fulfilled at the close of Christ's thousand year reign upon the earth, but many Scriptures indicate that Christ's reign in His blessed humanity will extend over "nations" and "generations in the ages to come." See Rev. 21:24, and chapter 22:2.

If Satan has had such terrible sway over this earth for six thousand years, it seems unreasonable that the meek and lowly Jesus, as the heir of David, should reign on the earth only a thousand years. The millennial age will complete the plan of human redemption, and fulfill the requirements of the jubilee year, for the restitution of all lawful rights to this planet back to the new Adam and His redeemed ones.

But out and beyond the Ages of Christ's theocratic dominion will sweep the measureless flow of the blessed Father's administration, in which there will be no delegated authority, but every creature in the circle of a holy creation will be lovingly swayed by the blessed Godhead, and have open vision of the Eternal Father, Son, and Holy Ghost. Then will come to pass the prayer, "Our Father who art in Heaven, Thy kingdom come."

CHAPTER 15

HOLY GHOST TEARS

Tears are both natural and spiritual; that is, we may shed tears from purely natural causes, without any reference to spiritual conditions or moral character, but as a mere effusion of natural feelings, which may be naturally bad as well as naturally good.

When the Holy Spirit begins to operate on the soul, the mind will act on the body, and frequently produce weeping. Tears which are shed as a result of the operation of the Spirit may be called in a certain sense Holy Ghost tears.

Tears have a language just as definite and emphatic as smiles or gestures. Words do not constitute the only language we speak, for everywhere there are many languages spoken by every human being. There is a language in our gait, our tones of voice, our eyes, smiles, gestures, and physical movements, and in our laughter, or facial expression, or our tears.

These all form so many avenues through which the inner personal soul expresses itself outwardly. The Holy Spirit unites Himself to the human spirit, imparting Divine ideas and Divine feelings, and these are expressed more or less by the action of the mind on the body.

The Bible is full of tears. See how the patriarchs "lifted up their voices and wept;" read the prophets, how the tears poured down their cheeks night and day; go through the New Testament, and see Jesus weeping with His friends at the grave of Lazarus; read Paul's Epistles, where the burning tears fell on the page as he wrote. What a vast ocean of heart life and pathos and feeling pervades the whole Bible! It is not a stoical, human, philosophical book; it throbs with deep feeling from beginning to end. It is a wonderful blessing to any human soul to have the Holy Ghost plow up the deep, interior fountains, and melt all the emotions, and cause the heart to pour itself out in tears.

When tears are shed under deep religious feelings, they

always clarify the mind and cause us to see all things in a clearer and more heavenly light. It would seem that as the salt tears wash the physical eye, there is a corresponding mental effect, and that the eye of the mind is cleansed to see things far off and in a stronger light. This clarifying of the mind, which comes from weeping, does not trouble the mind or leave the inward spirit perturbed, but it spreads through the soul a delightful and unspeakable serenity, like the shining tranquility which we often see in nature after a heavy shower of rain.

There are five kinds of Holy Ghost tears.

1. Those tears which we shed over our natural miseries; even though such tears seem to be purely human, yet the Holy Spirit can blend with them and utilize them to spiritual ends. When we see the rapid changes of life, the passing away of friends, the universal dilapidation and unhappiness of mankind, the multiplied sorrows that come into human life, and cause us to weep over the vision of such things, God can turn it to a good account and make such weeping the ministry of repentance and the call to prepare for another world.

2. Those tears which flow from conviction of sin, especially when we see the sin in the light of God and look at it in contrast with the Divine compassion and longsuffering toward us. All truth, to be forcible, must be seen with its two sides as a whole and not as a half truth. And so the sight of our sins, or of sin in general, would not of itself break up the deep of the heart into weeping. But when this vision of sin is seen in connection with God's longsuffering and compassion toward us, and we get a little glimpse into the tenderness and merciful feeling of God for sinners, then the sin seems heart breaking. And so the conscience is touched to the quick, and the conscience acts on the mind, and the mind in direct connection with the brain and nervous system, which, being excited by the spiritual feelings, produces a flow of tears.

It was this kind of weeping that Mary Magdalene poured out over the feet of her precious Lord; it was this kind of tears that flowed thick and fast from the eyes of Peter when he heard the cock crow. No sinner can be made to weep by a mere, cold, formal sight of his sins. Mt. Sinai made the Jews tremble, but it did not make them weep. And so the denunciation of sin, or the portrayal of it, can never of itself produce penitential tears. It is only when the sins are seen under the soft, melting light of infinite pity and love, that the heart is broken and the tears flow. Law may reveal sin, but nothing in the universe except love will make a man hate his sins. Water may be locked up in ice, but you cannot drink it till it is melted, and it takes the warmth of the tenderest love to bring forth the waters of repentance.

3. There are tears of a higher degree, which flow from spiritual meditation, such as long and clear contemplation of the sufferings of Jesus, of the poverty and trials, the self-abnegation and the boundless charity shown us in His life and death. And also in connection with this the contemplation of other innocent sufferers, such as the martyrs, and the great trials that God's holy and humble ones have passed through in their humility and innocence.

Sinners will shed many tears over pathetic scenes in novels or as acted on the stage. But such tears do not arise from the conscience or the moral faculties, but only on the surface, without producing any religious fruit. These tears of this third class are similar, in the spiritual life, to these superficial tears shed by the novel reader, only they are on a much higher scale, and produced from spiritual fountains within the heart. And they lead to very blessed fruit in grace, for such tears cause us to appreciate the sufferings of Jesus, and they give us a feeling of kinship with the suffering saints in all the ages.

4. The tears we shed out of an intense desire of seeing God, of beholding Jesus. These are tears of a still higher order. These are tears such as David shed when he longed for the courts of the living God during his banishment, and when he said his soul thirsted for God as the panting hart after the water brooks. These are the tears Mary shed when she sat at the empty tomb of Jesus, with an unspeakable longing to find her dear Lord, whom she supposed they had taken away.

There are no tears that give us such a deep and beautiful insight into the preciousness of Christ's person and character as these tears of holy longing. When we get an opportunity for long seasons of secret prayer, and pour out our hearts in every detail to our Heavenly Father, and then leave ourselves open for the Spirit to work in us as He pleases, and He begins to draw us out in pure, heart longings after God, it is glorious beyond description to have Him give us glimpses of Himself that seem to entice our souls almost out of the body, and draw us away with such inward pantings that the heart seems to leap and bound upward into the Heavenly world. We seem in spirit to be running with all our might to get closer to His blessed face, and at every bound it seems our hearts will break with spotless desires after the living God, till the great fountain of tears is broken up and they flow like hot salt streams down our cheeks, and the soul cries out, "O my Lord! my Love! Thou infinitely blessed, tender, precious God; when shall I see Thee in Thy glory, and when shall I drink myself full of Thine eternal blessedness!"

These tears give to our inner eyes telescopic visions into the beauties of God, as they are clustered and set forth in the meek and lowly Jesus. These are the tears of supernaturalists, and float us, like Noah's flood, above the highest mountain tops of earth, into the deep, blue dome of the peace and joy of God.

5. Another kind of spiritual tears are those we shed out of pure love for our fellows, when we weep over the sins of mankind, the calamities of our neighbors, and out of a heart sorrow for the salvation of souls. Such are the tears St. Paul shed over the wayward Galatians, and over those persons who had made shipwreck of their faith. It was tears like this that Samuel shed when the Lord told him that Saul had turned away from God, and was rejected from being king, and the great loving prophet wept all night long.

It was such holy, loving tears as these that fell from the eyes of Jesus as He sat on Mt. Olivet and looked over His beautiful but ill-fated Jerusalem, and said, while the tears trickled down His cheeks, "O Jerusalem, Jerusalem, how oft would I have gathered you, as a hen gathereth her chickens under her wings, and ye would not." These were the kind of tears the weeping prophet, Jeremiah, poured out all his life over the sins and desolations of his people. These are the tears that soul-winners who are filled with holy love shed over the souls that they are seeking to save. These are the Holy Ghost tears which the humble and holy ones pour out in the silent night watches before God, over the awful backslidings in the churches, over worldly ministers, and cold, lifeless congregations.

Perhaps these tears take us down deeper in the heart of Jesus, because they bring us into the plan of His sacrifice for others, and knit us in sympathy with His soul over the lost. There are many professed Christians who seldom weep; in fact, many of them speak slightingly of tears, but such persons are leagues away from the true Bible life. May God pity the dry-eyed Christians, for if the eye is dry, the heart behind the eye is dry also.

We must never have self-complacency in our tears, or look upon them as good in themselves. They are simply the effect, which proves the working of a deep spiritual cause, back in the soul. But while we are not to be attached to our tears, we are to thank God that He gives them to us. Above all things, we are to seek that inward tenderness of nature, that lowly contrition of heart, that interior union with the Christ-life, out of which Holy Ghost tears may flow.

CHAPTER 16

ANXIETY AND FAITH

There are many things we can study to great advantage in the notice of their contrasts; in fact, there are some things that are difficult to apprehend except by studying them negatively; by finding what they are not, our minds are aided in grasping what they are.

Anxiety and faith are just the opposite of each other, and by looking at them contrastively we may get deeper insights to both and be aided in losing the one and acquiring the other.

1. Anxiety has its center in the creature, but faith has its center in God. Everything has a center to it, and this applies to mental and moral principles as truly as to forms of matter or living things. Anxiety could never form a part of the experience of an immortal soul unless it were in some way depending on created beings or things. Reason is the parent of anxiety, for when reason does not act under the guidance of the Holy Spirit it invariably leads to distrust of some kind. Reason looks at the creature, at friends or foes, at circumstances and probabilities, at laws of nature and the prospects. And seeing only the realm of the natural it can never produce perfect confidence.

On the other hand faith pierces through all creatures, and all circumstances, and fastens itself upon an infinite, universal God, Who is in all, and through all, and who knows all and superintends all. Faith is the eye of the human spirit looking at God; and, in a certain lofty sense, ignoring everything but God.

That incomprehensible invention known as the X-ray will pierce through planks, or hundreds of pages of paper, or any amount of flesh, and reveal the center of every object the first of all, so that the observer looking through the lens sees the bones of a man before he sees the flesh. This beautifully illustrates the principles of inspired faith. It pierces through the thick walls of circumstance and phenomena and sees God, first of all, reposing at the center of all events and beings, and looks at other things as they are related to God. If thoughtful persons will stop to examine every anxious feeling they have had, and trace it to its starting point, they will find it is centered in some creature and not in the Creator.

2. Anxiety originates in the wants of a fallen state, but faith has its origin in the fulness of the provisions of God. If it had not been for the fall of man the human mind would never have been tortured with anxiety. There never would have been any abnormal or fictitious wants, but only such legitimate needs as the Creator found, and these would have met a counterpart supply without the intervention of foreboding or questioning fears.

The fallen condition of the soul makes it have many overreaching desires and an excessive feeling of want, as a raging fever produces many abnormal wants in a sick person. The reason is busy with these wants and is constantly searching for ways and means to gratify them. And in doing this it sees only the chances of human life. It sees the thousands of instances where these wants are not supplied, and this creates anxiety. Furthermore, the more these wants are brooded upon the more exhorbitant they grow until the natural life becomes a series of multiplied wants.

On the other hand faith goes out from the creature and looks upon the fulness of God. It searches into His character, His benevolence, His inexhaustible fulness to supply the mind and affections, and sees in ever widening oceans not only the resources of God, but His loving willingness to supply His creatures. This interior vision of the fulness of God destroys anxiety.

The very looking at our wants, unless it be through the fulness of God's supply, will produce anxiety. We often multiply our wants by looking at them, and faith alone can counteract this principle of distress; for just as our fallen state makes shortsighted reason its ally, so faith is God's ally in the soul, and it alone can rest in the fulness of God.

3. Anxiety is bounded by the vision of the natural perceptions and is attached to things around it. But faith has a wonderful expansiveness to it, and is attached to God's will wherever that will may be found anywhere in the universe.

The natural reason is nearsighted and sees things only that

affect the present hour and emergency. It sees things fragmentary, and so is perplexed at the mishaps and complications of men and things. It attaches itself to this or that thing or enterprise, and when there is a collapse or disappointment it is in consternation.

On the other hand faith is long-visioned and is expanded wherever God exists. It is firmly attached to His will, so that it does not cling to any creature, or circumstance, or nation, or human creed, or church, or earthly props. It is internally united to God Himself, and thus it can use the present order of the world without abusing it, and easily let go of all things and circumstances to follow God. St. Peter, describing the fulness of the graces, says, "he that lacks these graces is blind and near-sighted, so that he cannot see afar off."

Anxiety is near-sighted, but faith has a telescopic vision and sees things afar off. Faith looks at passing events from the standpoint of eternity, as they will appear a thousand years hence. Hence anxiety results from seeing all creatures and events out of their proper proportion. It sees things to be giants which faith, looking at in the light of eternity, regards only as tiny insects.

4. Anxiety is always changing its objects, but faith has no change of object, and its only change is to increase and intensify. Human reason, which is the instrument of anxiety, fixes its hope first on this person, then on that, first on this party or government, or enterprise, or prospect, and then on that.

Hence anxiety is like a person crossing a river of floating blocks of ice, stepping on this one hoping it will float them over, but finding that it is melting or sinking they step on another. And so all through life the mind never reaches a solid repose.

On the other hand faith has gotten down through the shifting sands on the earth's surface and is anchored in the primeval rock of God and His Word. It never changes its object and has no desire to change, for resting in an infinite God it spurns even the thought of change. There is no need of any change in the blue dome of the sky, or the white light of the sun, or the blue waves of the sea, or the laws of gravitation, because these things are all sufficient. And as the birds in the sky, and the fish in the sea have no thought of wanting a change in the constitution of the sky or sea, so when faith has found its abiding place in God it never dreams of wishing to change its object but will, to all eternity, find its sufficiency in Him. And the more it expands and apprehends God, the farther it gets from ever wanting to change the center of its rest.

5. Anxiety, resulting from various reasonings, is always manifold and complex, and divided into many forms and things, but faith is united and simple. Human reason is constantly making excursions into things curious. It experiments with heresy and all kinds of false doctrines under the deceitful pretense of finding the truth.

Professed Christians who think they have perfect faith in God manifest a religious anxiety by quizzing into the antichrist theories of second probation, annihilation, conditional immortality, the restoration of devils, Swedenborgian denial of the resurrection, Christian Science, mind reading, higher criticism, the mere moral theory of the atonement, physical immortality before death, holiness by keeping the Jewish law, and other unscriptural theories. These are complex and soul puzzling, producing only an argumentative state of mind and a feverish state of the heart, showing that the whole system of their religion had dragged its anchor from pure faith in God to the fluctuating sands of reason.

When the believer has been crucified, until not one trace of selfishness or self-will remains, God Himself then becomes the only object of His unchanging faith. The three persons of the Godhead are fountains of unchangeable comfort and peace. And perfect faith in God unites all other principles of the mind in quietness and harmony like the seven colors that are united in a ray of pure light.

Perfect faith in God is a miracle of simplicity and reduces all things in life to a state of simplicity. The reason, the judgment, the affections, the words, the labors of such a soul move in straight lines under the dominion of a supernatural and simple faith which in everything shuns the complex and seeks for the plain and transparent. Hence we notice people whose religion is mixed up, and who are trying to live by their reason, are always uneasy. There is a chronic distress in their lives, a vacillation in their service for God, and a fruitless effort to find happiness in somebody or something apart from God Himself. But perfect faith in God has a sweet satisfaction in it. It drinks continually from the sun bright fountains of God Himself through the person of Christ and by the indwelling of the Holy Spirit.

If a little pool of water should get its eye on the dry air, and the cloudless sky, and the dusty earth, it might faint under the thought of drying up and be in deep distress. But if it could see the ocean and perceive the constant evaporation of millions of tons of moisture going up in the air, its anxiety about drying up would pass away. Thus the soul that in perfect faith gazes on the ocean of God is kept from uneasiness and inward distress of heart, for it lives on what it sees in God and not on the appearance of things.

6. The principle of reason is always struggling to achieve results, but the principle of faith accomplishes the greatest results by harmonizing with God and working through Him. Not only are unsaved people full of anxiety, but great multitudes who are serving God allow their reason to take the place of faith. And so the churches, the camp meetings, the Christian conventions and missions present a scene of so much human planning, and wire pulling, and partiality, and cliques, and sets, and boards where half believing or make-believing people are taxing their wits with policy and plans and fears to bring things to pass, as they think, for the glory of God. But when they are tried in the fire, or ground to powder, there is hardly an ounce of faith found to a ton of rubbish of reasonings and anxieties.

Pure faith sinks itself into God, seeks only His will regardless of apparent success or failure— it works through the Holy Ghost and lets God bring about results. When the soul is made one with God by pure faith it achieves things in a Divine way, and in the Divine time, free from anxiety and free from the arduous struggles of the natural mind. Perfect faith sees God in a failure, or a smash up, where other people regard everything as a total wreck.

Thus all through life anxiety sprouts from the creature and makes its home in human reason and calculations. But faith springs up in union with God, anchors fast to the Eternal Will, feeds itself on God's unchanging love, and keeps tranquil in the all-hidden presence of God. It has no interest in the outcome of anything except the interest of God, and seeks in all things to be one with Jesus Christ. And in that union, anxiety can find no foothold.

CHAPTER 17

THRESHING OUT CHAFF

There are several references in Scripture to threshing out chaff, separating it from the wheat, as a type of a spiritual and disciplinary process of separating the fruit of Divine grace from the excrescencies, superfluities, and various defects of human nature.

Chaff is not a type of sin, because it is something essential to the growing of the grain. But for the chaff, a grain of wheat or corn could never be grown. But it is a something that, after serving a temporary purpose, is not only no longer needed, but is good for nothing except to be burned or utilized for manure. In the growing of grain, weeds, briars, and grass are Scripture emblems of sinful dispositions that choke the growing grain and need plowing out and purging away. But the chaff is an essential protection to the young grain in its milk state, and must not be removed till the grain is ripe. These facts in nature have their exact counterpart in grace.

If we trace out this thought about separating the chaff from the matured corn, it will explain many experiences in the sanctified life which have perplexed many souls. Every principle of Divine grace and providence has a manifold application to nations, churches, and individuals. This law of threshing out chaff from the golden grain has a broad, universal application, and also extends down into all the particulars of our individual lives.

1. Apply this to the Church of Christ at large. The Scriptures teach that God's true people in the earth, those who are born of the Holy Spirit and living a life of prayer and obedience and seeking to be holy, are the true Church of God. This Church is living amid the different political and civil governments of the world, and these forms of civil government are the providential appointments of God for the present age, and are essential to the social, educational, moral, and commercial welfare of man-

kind. Nevertheless, these governments of human authority are only temporary arrangements, like the chaff to protect the religious liberties and interests of the living Church while it is in the green milk stage of this present dispensation.

When the "Church of the first born" has been completed, and the individual grains of wheat have all been ripened by the Holy Ghost, then Jesus will come at the end of the Age, for the Greek says "the harvest is the end of the Age," not the end of the world. That will be the threshing out time, when the wheat of the true Church will be separated from the chaff of all mere human institutions. Then the earthly governments will go to pieces and be, Daniel tells us, "as the chaff of the summer threshing floor;" and the wheat, who are the true saints, will take the kingdom and reign with their Head and Lord.

Now, if you search the Scriptures through with this key thought in your mind about the wheat and the chaff you will find scores of passages that fit into it exactly. This is the application of Daniel 2:31-35, and of Matt. 13:1-12, and of Romans 13:1-4.

God is dealing with the Church at large as a great unit, as an individual, and carries out through the slow, creeping centuries His discipline over the Church of the first born the same way that He deals with an individual Christian, till they "all come unto a perfect man."

2. Apply this principle of threshing out chaff to us personally. This is what Paul does in Romans 5:1-5 in which he teaches us that we are first "justified by faith," and then after that "have access by faith into established grace," and then after our sanctification we are put through a process of "tribulation." The word tribulation is from "tribulum;" that is a flail which the ancient Romans used to beat out the ripened grain and separate the wheat from the chaff. Now notice that this tribulum could never be used on grain until it had reached a point of perfection, and was thoroughly dry, so the chaff could be separated from it.

Now, there is a great deal of chaff closely enfolded around our spiritual lives which does not consist in things positively sinful, and which in many respects are needful to protect the weak and milk stages of religious life, and which if removed too soon would overtax our courage and faith and love and be our spiritual ruin. Hence, we must be sanctified and anointed with the Holy Ghost, and weaned from the milk state of grace, and ripened in the hot sunshine of Divine truth, before we are prepared for the tribulum, that is, God's providential threshing machine, to take the chaff from us, that we may be all pure wheat and prepared for the coming age. Among the things which make up the chaff that is to be threshed out of a sanctified soul, we may enumerate the following:

Unwise zeal. Real zeal is most essential to a Christian life, but it must have an expression through the judgment. Though the heart may be pure, the judgment may be weak or immature, and so the zeal may be at times very unwise and overdo a thing or underdo it. Yet even if this unwise zeal were utterly taken from a freshly sanctified soul it would be his ruin, and with all the mishaps and awkwardness of expression it is essential to the life and progress of the soul. After a while the work of tribulation will chasten the judgment and separate the superfluity without destroying the golden grain of pure zeal. This is a high art which God alone is equal to.

Error in the knowledge of Scriptures. No Christian has ever lived who did not have to correct, or enlarge, or rearrange his theology after the experience of sanctification. The word theology is made of two Greek words, *"theos"*-- God, and *"logos,"*-- a word, or reason, or understanding; hence, theology is our view or reason concerning God.

There are many systems of theology written out by men, but there is no system of theology written out of earth that embodies all the varied experiences of a perfect believer. Now, if all the real Christians on earth should have their theology, whether Catholic or Protestant, Calvinistic or Arminian, taken from them, it would be their religious ruin. But after souls are baptized with the Holy Ghost, and the spiritual life strengthens all the mental faculties, then the Lord's tribulum begins to work. By sore trials and awful temptations the understanding is marvelously sharpened, the mind is lifted into a sweep of vision where it can comprehend Scripture on a broader generalization, and analyze fine points of experience, and discover the character of God, in such a way as to eliminate many an old tradition or false teaching which hitherto was held sacred.

In many cases the close communionist sees his unscriptural narrowness, and the rigid Calvinist discovers he must "make his own election sure," and the intense Arminian sees his nothingness and finds himself adoring God's sovereign purposes, and the medicine man discovers that Jesus is a healer of diseases, and the man who thought the Gospel would convert the world discovers everywhere in Scripture that Jesus must return and chain Satan in the pit and conquer the nation in order to bring the millennium. And a great many other theological notions are rectified, enlarged, and flooded with heavenly light, and much theological chaff is burned up or blown to the winds.

This is one of the experiences that Job passed through in the deeper crucifixion, for though God affirmed that he was a perfect man, yet the theology of his day was that perfect loyalty to God would always be rewarded with temporal prosperity. Job's three friends clung to that old theology, but the Lord destroyed that chaff out of Job's faith by the tribulation he went through.

Some form of theology is absolutely essential to every Christian, but the very imperfection of our nature involves some chaff in religious thinking, and should this chaff be taken away too soon it might damage the faith. Only when the faith is perfect can the erroneous chaff be threshed out.

Our work an unconscious idol. A soul perfect in love must work; it loves to work and its work will be attended with success, and then there grows in the heart, more rapidly than the soul is aware, a creature attachment to the work.

See how sanctified people will become intensely devoted to their religious enterprises, their camp meeting, their mission, their paper, their way of holding a meeting, their singing. And when the Lord allows their favorite work to be hindered, or when some one else is allowed to take it, see what a terrible ordeal it is for them to go through. But this is the way God threshes out the chaff of undue attachment to our religious work. Sometimes souls are not able to bear this threshing process, and when God would wean them from their own work, they sulk, or despair, and give up doing anything. This well tests the genuineness of one's sanctification, for attachment to God is pure wheat, but a creature attachment to our work is chaff, yet who has the grace to believe it.

Human sweetness of religious friendship. Divine grace vitalizes, refines, and intensifies all our natural affections. In fact many people seem greatly lacking in adequate natural affection until they are melted clean through by the baptism with the Holy Ghost. Then the soul forms new attachments and friendships with great zest, and yet the human sweetness and fervor of these friendships may become a snare. Hence the necessity of a chastening, a weaning, a process of threshing, that the chaff element in these religious friendships may be purged away. This is a very painful process, and cuts human love to the quick, but the sanctified soul is thus crucified even to the saints, and all its attachments must be dissolved in the Holy Spirit, and celestialized, to reach everlasting fixedness in God.

Phenomena and forms of experience. There are many forms of experience under the first gushes of the Spirit's baptism like a drenching spring rain, which after a while change into more noiseless and interior operations. With changes comes bewilderment to the newly sanctified heart, for there is unconsciously some religious chaff in depending on our own experiences, and too much of the creature in enjoying spiritual emotions, and lights, and inner voices, and heavenly dreams, which renders it expedient for tribulation to thresh out, that we may love the three persons in the Godhead instead of loving our experiences.

There is also chaff in most cases in our manners, and voices, and gestures. Often times the very buoyancy of a fresh religious experience makes a person act rude and imprudent and boisterous, which requires many a thump, or providential snubbing, or brotherly rebuke, to bring the soul into modest restraint, and thoughtfulness of behavior, and to practice the fitness of things. Much chaff is in the form of fanciful, extravagant and impracticable religious schemes.

How many fully consecrated souls think of filling the world with their great enterprises, and are so carried away with their pious schemes as to neglect secret prayer and doing the duty at hand. God must send His threshing machine in the shape of failures, and manifold weaknesses, and disappointments, to take the chaff out of such persons and sober them down to a humble, patient walk with God.

These are only a few items that make up the chaff which tribulation must thresh out even from sanctified souls. They are not sins, but spiritual superfluities, in many instances needful to help weak nature, but in a mature state of pure love are hindrances. Still in threshing these things out there must be many a pain, many a tear, many a heartache, many a lonely hour of desolate feeling.

This is the deeper death in the Christian life, through which the soul must pass in order to reach the fulfillment of the Divinely prompted longings of grace. When this chaff is threshed out, all the faculties of the soul become as pure as gold and enter into a deep, sweet, solid, inexpressible union with the person of God. There is a sinking into a limitless sea of love, of charitable feelings, of kind thinking, of holy contemplation of the Divine perfections, which is truly the apostolic state of grace.